"This book will challenge you to examine your priorities. It will challenge you to live as though you can make a difference, because you can. It will inspire you to share your hope as God wants you to, as Charles Mulli is doing."

HENRY TESSMANN
CEO Concordia Hospital, Winnipeg, Canada

"On a continent struggling to cope with fifteen million children orphaned from HIV/AIDS it is comforting to know there are people like the Mulli family who are willing to sacrifice all. This story of a rags-to-riches-to-father of hundreds of street children makes you hold your breath on page one and not release it until the end."

JANINE MAXWELL
Hopes and Dreams Team

"I fully expect that future historians of Kenya will say that the greatest single impact made on the young leaders of Kenya was by Charles and Esther Mulli through the agency of MCF. I wholeheartedly endorse this life changing, dynamic biography about the life and ministry of one of the finest couples I have ever met."

REV. JACK HAWKINS
Former Missions Director, Crossroads Missions

"Charles has indeed heard and responded to his Master's call of 'follow me.' This he has done despite being ostracized by the community and friends—a price few people would want to pay. He defied all odds. He is an entrepreneur who has converted his skills and knowledge to the betterment of lives of others through agriculture and the technical trades."

PROF. PETER B. KIBAS
Director, Kenya Institute of Management School

"I have discovered that Charles Mulli is a man, who dared to obey the Words of Jesus Christ literally—'Go your way, sell whatever you have and give to the poor' (Mark 10:21). Today we can see the result of his obedience as hundreds have found a place of love and care."

REV. CURT JOHANSSON
Founder of Maranatha Faith Assemblies, Kenya
International Director Trosgnistan Mission, Sweden

"I knew Mr. Mulli's commitment to God when we met to discuss the Mully Children's Family in Eldoret, in the early 1990s. He was a troubled man who wanted to do everything possible to respond to the needy children's plight. When I see what has happened in the lives of many children who have passed through his hands, I know he is a true servant of God."

MARGARET BASIGWA
Deputy Director of Children's Services
Ministry of Home Affairs and National Heritage, Kenya

To contact the **Mully Children's Family Home:**

Email: mcfhomes@africaonline.co.ke
or mcf@mullychildrensfamily.org

Website: www.mullychildrensfamily.org

FATHER TO THE FATHERLESS

The Charles Mulli Story

PAUL H. BOGE

Father to the Fatherless: The Charles Mulli Story
Copyright ©2005 Paul H. Boge
Printed in Canada

June, 2005	*February, 2009*	*August, 2011*	*May, 2015*
June, 2006	*May, 2009*	*May, 2012*	
February, 2007	*September, 2009*	*July, 2012*	
April, 2008	*November, 2009*	*April, 2013*	
August, 2008	*June, 2010*	*February, 2014*	

International Standard Book Number: 978-1-89721-302-5

Published by:
Castle Quay Books
19-24 Laguna Pkwy, Lagoon City, Brechin, Ontario, L0K 1B0
Tel: (416) 573-3249
E-mail: info@castlequaybooks.com   www.castlequaybooks.com

Copy editing by Essence Publishing
Cover Design by Garth Armstrong
Cover Photo by Reynold Mainse
Printed at Essence Publishing, Belleville, Ontario

All Scripture quotations, unless otherwise specified, are from the *Revised Standard Version* of the Bible (Copyright © 1946, 1952; © 1971, 1973 by the Division of Christian Education of the National Council of the Churches of Christ in the United States of America.) • Scripture marked MSG taken from *The Message*, copyright © by Eugene H. Peterson, 1993, 1994, 1995. Used by permission of NavPress Publishing Group.

Library and Archives Canada Cataloguing in Publication
Boge, Paul H., 1973-
    Father to the fatherless: the Charles Mulli story / Paul H. Boge.
ISBN 978-1-89721-302-5

    1. Mulli, Charles. 2. Mully Children's Family. 3. Orphans--
Services for--Kenya. 4. Street children--Services for--Kenya.
5. Abandoned children--Services for--Kenya. 6. Children of AIDS
patients--Services for--Kenya. 7. Christian biography--Kenya.
8. Kenya--Biography. I. Title.

HV28.M84B63 2005   362.73'2'096762   C2005-902375-9

ACKNOWLEDGEMENTS

God—for Your love that knows no boundaries: from the richest of the rich to the abject poorest of the poor; and for Your power that truly changes lives.

Charles Mulli—for entrusting me with the task of writing your story and for living a life that has impacted people throughout the world.

Charles Mulli's family—Mrs. Esther Mulli, Jane, Miriam, Grace, Ndondo, Kaleli, Mueni, Isaac and Dickson for your friendship and for your invaluable help in going over the drafts.

MCF supporters around the world—you have given tirelessly to this ministry. Your ongoing support makes this rescue ministry possible.

Larry Willard—my publisher, for taking on this project and for your passion in getting this story told.

Bruce Wilkinson—for your encouragement and for writing the foreword.

Endorsers—for your thoughtful supporting comments.

Stephanie Webb and Elfrieda Balzer—for your dedicated editing help and encouragement with this story.

My family—Hans, Lorna, Hans, Tanya, Maya, Arianna, Hans Lukas, Elora, Randy, Heidi, Omi Boge and Oma Baerg for your constant support and for sharing the vision of MCF.

Janine Maxwell—for our friendship that began at MCF, and for your support in this book.

Garth Armstrong—for creating a captivating cover design.

To my prayer partners—Uwe, Christoph and Harry, for the countless times you have prayed for me and for your undying dedication to building His kingdom.

To you the reader—for supporting the ministry through this book.

And to all the children of MCF—for proving there are no lost causes and that nothing is impossible to those who believe.

FOREWORD

This book is breathtaking from the first page. As I read it, I was torn between wanting to read faster to see what was going to happen and putting it down because I could easily forecast what the next page held for the small child named Charles. This book is not for the faint of heart, but it is for those who have a heart for the truth. The truth about the human spirit, the truth about the will to live and the truth about God's unending love for those "overlooked or ignored" (Matthew 25:45 MSG).

It is an anomaly to see selflessness in action in 2005. Even those of us, who believe God has given us all we have, struggle with the thought of giving it all up if He asked us to. The Mulli family did just that. They live in daily obedience to the call.

We live in a time of extreme wealth and excess. *Father to the Fatherless* forces us to leave our daily trials and live for a moment in the world that fifteen million African children are living in today, abandoned and alone with no hope for the future. Charles shows us that there is hope even where there seems to be no hope. Millions of North Americans today feel hopeless and helpless, but they are not alone. Whether we are surrounded by people and things or alone in a hut sitting beside a dying parent, the hurt is the same. Jesus came to ease the pain that we all feel. He is Hope for the Hopeless. He is Love for the Unloved. He is the Father to the Fatherless.

It is inspiring to read this story of one Kenyan family's commitment to helping save their country, one child at a time. Nelson Mandela is ONE person. Martin Luther King Jr. was ONE person. Mother Teresa was ONE person. Each of these individuals did so much to change the face of the world. *Father to the Fatherless* is a lesson to us all that one person really can change the future of a nation. You are ONE person. You can make a difference in the life of a child. Do it today. Don't delay because tomorrow will be too late.

BRUCE WILKINSON
Dream for Africa

Author's Introduction

It was dark. It was late. The children at the MCF home in Ndalani, Kenya had all gone to bed for the evening. I sat in a quiet room at a table across from Charles Mulli. I took notes as he recounted his life story and shook my head often in disbelief, trying to wrap my head around what I was hearing.

We know of rags-to-riches stories—people who start out at the bottom and surpass incredible odds. We cheer for them because, I think, we can relate to them, or at least to their struggle of climbing to the top. But Charles is much more than this. He took it a step further. Well, more than a step, really. He chose to do more than what was required. And I wanted to find out why.

Plus, I'm fascinated with miracles. I heard stories about what he had done. I heard about the healings. I even heard about the deliverances. Some think miracles are not for today—that they are from a forgotten era, like buried treasure better left unfound. Miracles, however, are not a strange world for people like Charles. It's the world they live in, because they have to if they are going to survive.

It's been said that Charles Mulli is not a man that people understand. Maybe it gets that way with those who walk so close with God. I've heard him referred to as "a friend of God." Those who know him would agree.

Life comes down to choices. We choose for or against Christ. And the reason I hold Charles in such high respect is not only that he made a one-time decision but that he continues to make the decision to follow Christ on a daily basis. I don't know that following Christ gets any easier with time. Maybe it's not supposed to. And for those that do, for people like Charles, the adventure becomes more and more powerful.

And so I took notes of his life over a number of days, mostly in the evening, in that room, in the dark, in the quiet. I listened as he started from the beginning and explained in detail the events that had shaped his incredible life.

This is what he told me.

CHAPTER 1

It was the worst time of day.

Six-year-old Charles Mulli lay awake in bed in his family's one-room thatched hut. It was late; he was tired; yet it was impossible for him to fall asleep. He kept as still as he could listening for any sign, any hint, of danger. Beside him his younger brothers lay sleeping, unaware of the potential for disaster. He heard his mother, Rhoda, in the bed next to him, breathing. Her inhaling and exhaling sounded laboured to Charles. He knew all too well she wasn't sleeping either. How could she?

Terror wasn't more than a heartbeat away.

Charles turned over in his bed, hoping somehow to rid himself of the panic beginning to grip his spirit. He felt his pulse start to pound in his neck. He tried to tell himself that everything would be all right, that tonight they would escape unharmed. But the thumping in his neck only grew stronger—as though it were an indication of what was about to happen. Every gust of wind, every sound of an animal was magnified a thousand times by his imagination. He chased those thoughts away, hoping instead to stay focused on listening for the sounds he was dreading to hear. A momentary peace came to him, a faint glimmer of hope that, perhaps, they were in the clear. The African night became quiet. Almost too quiet.

But all of that was about to change.

He wanted to ask his mother if she thought they were safe for the evening—hoping the tone of her voice would either confirm or deny his doubt of their chances to make it through the night in security. It was already past midnight. Certainly by now they were out of harm's way. Certainly they'd managed to sidestep horror tonight. Tomorrow? Yes, it would be the same suspense. And yes, eventually it would happen. Eventually they would have to live, or die, through the ordeal. But at least for now they could hang on to the hope that it wouldn't be them. That it wouldn't be tonight.

Charles wanted those reassuring words from his mother. The comforting touch that, in an instant, could bring him peace. But in his heart he wondered if she would give him the answer he wanted. She would not lie to her son. If she thought it was coming tonight she would tell him. Charles wanted to know his chances, her chances, of survival. But he decided not to ask her. He worried that any sound he made would break the fragile calm surrounding the penetrable Mulli home.

Maybe his father had been in a fight. Maybe tonight he had finally met his match and been beaten unrecognizable by fellow drunkards. Even though Daudi Mulli had successfully defended himself against as many as ten men in a fight before, he often stumbled into, or caused, altercations that nearly killed him. Perhaps tonight was one of those nights. That would explain his long delay in coming home. Or maybe Daudi was lying drunk on the side of the road, passed out after all the booze. Maybe he'd just gotten lost. Any of these would have been better for Rhoda, Charles and his brothers.

But that was not the case.

Daudi had been out drinking. As usual. And a lot. As usual. But he wasn't lying on the side of the road. He wasn't recovering from some beating in a fight. And he wasn't in the bar or trying to get into some brawl.

Daudi was on his way home.

It was Charles who heard him first. His father's shouting and slurring was unmistakable. Charles' instinctive reaction was to pretend what he heard wasn't real, that somehow his mind was projecting his worst fears into his consciousness. The pounding in his throat grew stronger. It wasn't him. It just couldn't be. Couldn't be.

But as much as Charles wished it were someone else, he knew who was approaching the hut. And he knew what was about to happen.

Rhoda sat up on her bed. She waited those paralyzing few moments before Daudi came to the door. He often fell to the ground on the way up to the hut. That was a good thing. Rhoda would go out, drag him into their home and lay him down in bed in his unconscious state. They preferred this option to other times, when Daudi came home drunk and, of course, violent. She waited for the sound of him crumpling to the ground. She waited for his slurred shouting to stop. It was their only chance.

Instead, she saw the door open.

She shot a terrified look at Charles that told him to hide under the bed, as if doing so could somehow protect him from the evil about to enter. Charles grabbed his brothers, pulled them off the bed and pushed them underneath. One began to cry. Charles covered his mouth and crawled under the bed.

He looked at the door and could just make out his father's feet. Maybe he would leave. Maybe he would just close the door and fall down drunk in the field. Daudi, however, stood there, not saying anything. Not at first. Charles pulled his head further underneath the bed. His growing fear of his father was overcome by his overwhelming concern for his mother. If ten men were barely a match for Daudi, how much less was one mother? Every instant felt like a lifetime. Charles waited in the deafening silence until Daudi started shouting at Rhoda.

He couldn't understand what his father was saying—not that it mattered. The tone was enough. It only reinforced their worst fears. The man was both drunk and angry. And there was no one within shouting, or screaming, distance who could help.

Daudi cursed at his wife. Charles closed his eyes, hoping that by doing so he could make all of this go away. Rhoda said nothing. What could she say? Her feet twitched in anxiety. She backed up against the wall. Daudi shouted so loudly that it seemed like a direct connection between his voice and the part of their brains that registered fear.

And then everything went quiet. Charles listened in the still of the night. Then he heard the sickening sound of Rhoda's choking fill the hut. Her desperate gasps for air grew fainter. She wheezed as best she could to draw whatever air she could into her lungs. Charles looked out from under the bed. What he saw made him wish he had remained hidden.

Daudi, short and incredibly well-built, had grasped his hands around his wife's throat. He throttled her back and forth. Rhoda tried without success to pry his hands off. Spit came out of her mouth and flew in all directions. She stomped her feet on the ground, thrashing her body, desperate for a way to release his hold. Her breathing stopped. Her pale tongue hung out of her mouth. Her face vibrated as though some electric current was passing through it. Then Daudi threw her on to the bed. She crashed into the corner and turned her head away from him, panting for breath. A vile gasping sound echoed in Charles' ears.

Daudi screamed and swore, blaming her for everything he could think of. Their poverty? Her fault. His trouble finding work? Her fault. Their meagre living conditions? Her fault. Everything. Her fault.

Rhoda had been through this many times before, and she'd gotten better at the game with practice. In other beatings she'd tried to reason with him, tried to calm him down, tried to reassure him that things were about to get better. But hope always seemed to make him more angry.

There would be no point in reasoning with Daudi. Least of all now.

So Rhoda stayed in the corner, pretending to be unconscious even as she tried to gain control of her breathing. So far she had managed to live through yet another attack and was almost relieved that it might now be over. But a mother's instinct for survival extends beyond herself, and when she heard Daudi curse and swear about where the children were, she turned towards him. She sat up as best she could, hoping to divert his attention away from them.

Daudi went to the children's bed. He ripped off the covers. It was empty.

"Where are they?" he screamed. It was so loud that Charles shook with terror. His small hands trembled. He didn't know if it was better to stay hidden or to come out. What was better for him? What was better for his brothers? What was better for his mother? What would it take to calm Daudi down?

Daudi turned to Rhoda. She shrank back in fear. But her plot had worked. She'd managed to turn his demented attention away from the children and bring it back upon herself.

"Where are they?" he shouted over and over again. The answer was obvious, of course. There aren't many places to hide in a hut. But Daudi wasn't interested in the obvious. He was interested in a fight.

Charles peered out from under the bed. His father towered over him. Charles smelled the rank stench of booze and body odour. But the smell was nothing compared to what he was about to see.

In one powerful swing, Daudi slammed his massive right hand down onto Rhoda's face. There was a tremendous smacking sound. The force of the blow snapped her head back, much the way a boxer's head snaps back when dealt the knockout blow. Rhoda's body shook with pain. Her head crashed against the side of the mud hut. She tried to orient herself again, but the punishing strike to her head made it impossible for her to tell from which direction Daudi would deliver the next hit.

She saw the door. It was still open. She could make it out. Daudi was drunk. Maybe he wouldn't be able to catch her. But the children—she couldn't leave them. She stayed on the bed, her eyes still not able to focus, and decided to take her chances with her husband.

The next blow came directly across her face. Daudi slapped her so hard that not only did her face burn in agony but her neck cracked as she fell onto her bed. She had expected this second strike. There was never just one. But the first one was harder and more painful than in previous beatings, and it left her with no ability to prepare herself for the escalating onslaught.

Daudi grabbed Rhoda's hair and yanked her to within better striking range. She screamed in terror of what was about to happen. Like wounded prey before a roaring lion, she pleaded with her husband to stop. He screamed at her as spit flew out of his mouth and into her face. He formed his right hand into a fist and repositioned his left hand in her hair to keep her from moving. Charles' eyes grew wide.

Daudi smashed his fist into Rhoda's face. Her head jerked back. All she could see now were vague shadows now. As the longing for unconsciousness overwhelmed her, guilt for abandoning her children multiplied her agony. Daudi was about to deliver the next blow when suddenly Rhoda screamed. It was a different scream that filled the hut, one Charles had never heard. It was a piercing shrill. She screamed from more than just pain. A terrible panic filled her voice, as she sensed, perhaps, that something unseen had just entered the hut. Her high-pitched voice carried with it the conviction that the hut was now enveloped by a presence none of them had previously encountered.

Daudi drilled Rhoda with another punch. It caught her half on the nose and half under her left eye. Blood spurted from her mouth. Her screaming stopped momentarily.

Charles' attempts to keep from crying failed. Even at six years old he knew the horrid ramifications of showing emotion during a beating. It was a sign of weakness, a sign of remorse, an outward indication that what Daudi was doing was wrong. Whatever it was, it enraged Daudi.

He let go of Rhoda, who crumpled like a dead woman onto the bed. He turned his face to Charles. He took a step towards him. Charles saw his mother's blood on his father's knuckles. He looked up his arm to his face. And what he saw shocked him. No doubt, it was his father standing there. But those eyes—they weren't his. There was something vicious in them.

Daudi crouched down and looked into the face of his boy. Charles' hands rattled. His neck pounded.

"Why are you crying?" he shouted.

That was a problem. Any answer—or no answer—was certain to be wrong. Charles said nothing.

"Why are you crying?" he screamed again. Daudi dragged Charles out from under the bed. That's when Daudi heard the other boys crying as well. In a fury he knelt down on the ground, reached under the bed and dragged out his other sons. They screamed and cried, covering their heads with their arms as though they were soldiers expecting a grenade to explode.

And the beating continued.

Charles was nearest. He would get it first. He looked up at his father and waited for the inevitable. The man he knew during sober times was nowhere to be found. Now, instead, Daudi had been replaced with something, or someone, else. He raised his hand to his ear. Charles saw it coming and tried to get out of the way. The blow struck Charles in the face with such force that his body spun around.

"Stop your crying!" Daudi shouted. Charles crawled onto his bed. Daudi grabbed him by the shoulders and threw him off the bed. Charles crashed against the mud wall and hit the ground, knocking the wind out of him.

Rhoda opened her eyes and saw her husband standing over the body of her oldest son.

"Stop," she said, in a voice that was so pathetic, so quiet, that it came out sounding more like an admission of defeat than a confident plea to stop this chaos.

Daudi hit each of the younger brothers, sending their tiny bodies spinning onto the ground. He grabbed Charles by the shoulders and stood him up. He spit in his son's face and then threw him against the wall. Charles crumpled to the ground, unable to cry. He wanted to protect his mother from the monster hitting at will in their cramped hut, but he had no strength. His mouth was covered in blood. His teeth stung with an unbearable pain.

Daudi turned back to Rhoda, who had been reduced to nothing more than a bloodied collection of skin and bones. No strength. No will. Just a faint heartbeat to differentiate her from the dead.

But the beatings had managed to exhaust Daudi. He stood there panting and then sat down on the bed next to his wife. Daudi stared ahead as if in a trance. He lay down beside his wife, oblivious to what he had done, and fell asleep.

Charles waited until it was safe to get up from the ground. Only then did he realize the incredible shooting pain at the back of his head. He felt dizzy. His eyes had a brutal time focusing. He wiped his mouth and felt the blood that had begun to dry. He looked over at his mother. She was breathing. But he avoided looking at his father as he got back into bed with his brothers. They were breathing, too. Thankfully, Rhoda and Charles had taken the brunt of the beating. Perhaps their presence had saved the younger ones.

Charles was the last to fall asleep—or unconscious, as the case may be. And as he drifted off he felt what little relief he could that they were done. They were in the clear. At least for now.

But unbeknown to all of them, the evening had just begun.

CHAPTER 2

Charles woke up in a panic. His heart raced. He gasped in a breath of air. He felt disoriented as his eyes began to adjust. He heard shouting in the distance. He assumed it was nothing, maybe just his imagination acting up after a beating, and tried to go back to sleep.

But before the night was finished he would wish that he had somehow slept through what was about to happen.

He put his head back down, but the screams became louder. It wasn't his imagination. It wasn't a dream, either. Sometimes a person wakes up from a frightening dream and feels the relief that comes with discovering it isn't reality. But in this case, Charles woke up from a dream and entered into a nightmare.

Daudi had his back against the door. His eyes and mouth were wide open. His white-coated tongue hung out. He gasped for breath in short, desperate bursts. Sweat poured off his face and dripped onto the ground. He smashed his head back and forth against the door as if to try to release himself from something.

Or from someone.

Charles looked down at the ground. Daudi's feet were barely touching it. His toes just made contact with the mud floor. He swung his fists at the air in front of him hoping somehow to stop whatever was attacking him.

It was as though some horrible, unseen figure was choking Daudi.

Rhoda woke up as well. Dried blood covered her bruised and barely recognizable face. She angled her head so that she could see with her left eye, which had not yet swollen shut. What she saw made her cringe and retreat to the corner.

The wheezing Daudi made became more intense. His laboured breathing had now turned into a serious struggle to get any, much less enough, air into his lungs. The wretched sounds coming from his mouth were those of a man about to die.

And both Charles and Rhoda wondered if that might not be the best thing for everyone.

Daudi dropped to the ground and clutched his throat as if doing so could somehow prevent the invisible terror from regaining control. He sucked in a deep breath. His chest heaved as he gasped for air. He stretched his hands out and pushed himself off the ground. A strange and momentary calm came to him.

And then it started again.

His body spun over in one violent, unnatural move, slamming his back onto the floor. The choking and wheezing started again—this time worse than before. It didn't sound human. Daudi wrapped his hands around his throat, trying to stop the assailant from squeezing the life out of him. He struggled left and right, but there would be no escape.

Charles stayed in his bed, overcome with anxiety about what would happen to his father—and what would happen to the rest of them once this force had finished Daudi off. They always had a chance against Daudi. They had survived him tonight. Maybe they could do it again. But there would be no defence against the evil presence in the room should Daudi die. How do you defend yourself against something you can't see?

Daudi coughed up blood as his eyes rolled to the back of his head. The air wasn't going in any more. The wheezing stopped. With violent thrusts Daudi smashed at anything within reach. His strength began to fail him, like a fighter who is too exhausted to continue a match.

And then, everything stopped.

The room went quiet.

And even though nothing else had changed, Charles and Rhoda felt the evil presence leave. Through the door, maybe. Or maybe back into thin air from which it came. Either way, it was gone—and they hoped it would stay away.

But it wouldn't be the last time Charles would encounter such a presence.

He looked at his father. Motionless. Perhaps dead. And both he and his mother wondered if this was a time to feel remorse or gratitude. He leaned forward to check on Daudi but then stopped, thinking that maybe the unseen force had invaded his father and would suddenly spring to life and attack him.

He heard his father begin to breathe. His eyes remained closed. He looked asleep. Charles looked at Rhoda, who had pushed herself into the corner. The tears stung the cuts on her face. He heard her weeping. It wasn't the sound of crying that says *things will get better; we're just going through a hard time.* These weren't even desperate tears, for even desperate tears have the hope that, somewhere, somebody knows her situation and will help. These were the tears of desolation. *This is my lot in life. This is the best that I will ever have.* She leaned her head against the wall in an awkward position. Lying down would be too painful. The trembling in her hands subsided. She drifted off.

Charles continued hearing his mother's screams in his mind. He felt the smash of his father's fist against his face over and over again. He saw the disgusting look on his father's face with his bulging eyes, his tongue sticking out as he lay on the ground gasping for breath. He worried about that sinister presence that was somewhere nearby, lurking about, ready to come back without any notice.

No. There would be no sleep tonight.

Not for Charles.

The night went on forever. Every sound, every gust of wind, brought with it the threat of new harm. Even the initial hints that dawn was approaching seemed surreal to him. The first ray of light brought him relief. They lived to see another day.

As the morning sun began to invade the Mulli hut it uncovered the treacherous events of the previous night. Charles saw the bruising on his arms. He tried to move his facial muscles and felt the sting on the sides of his head. He looked at his brothers, their faces strangely calm. No swelling. No bruises. Hardly any scratches.

His mother, however, was not so fortunate.

He saw a face that was almost unrecognizable. She was still crouched over in the corner as if subconsciously continuing to protect herself against an attack. Her body had sunk down somewhat during the course of the night. She looked like a burn victim. The sun cast light on the left side of her face, revealing the dark swelling. Spit dribbled from her fattened lip. Her hair stuck to patches of blood around her forehead.

And even though he wondered how terrible his own state might be, he tried instead, without success, to remember what his mother looked like without bruising. She seemed so frail, so abandoned. He didn't want her to wake up. Pain wouldn't hurt her nearly as much if she stayed asleep.

Daudi let out a heavy sigh. It scared Charles. His heart pounded. He froze, expecting his father to awake with violence. Daudi lay on his back, his hands sprawled over the bed. And then, as though being roused from the dead, he opened his eyes.

The monster was waking up.

Daudi let out a louder sigh. Even though Rhoda beside him had not woken up or gained consciousness, her mind already registered the sound. Her hands began to tremble, sensing the danger that was coming alive. Daudi sat up. His eyes focused. He looked around the room. The small table was cracked and lying on the floor. Beside him, crouched in the corner, was a woman neither he, nor anyone, could recognize. He turned his head to Charles.

They made eye contact.

A lightning bolt of fear shot through Charles. Daudi was within striking distance. He could smack Charles right now if he wanted to. Charles didn't know what to do. Should he look at his father? Would that only make things worse? Should he look away? Would that spurn his rage?

A puzzled expression came to Daudi's face, as though he was curious how something like this could have happened. He leaned forward for a closer look at Charles. Charles moved his head back, sucking in a deep breath, bracing himself for what he was sure would be a horrific crack.

But his father did nothing but stare. He looked at his son with indifference. He had no tears. No remorse. He'd been here before on the morning after. They'd all been here before. And as one who becomes calloused by the routine things in life, Daudi said nothing, got up and walked out the door.

As if that was her cue to wake up, Rhoda opened her one good eye and let the sunlight into her body. Another day. Another day in the Kenyan village of Kathithyamaa with no money, no husband and no hope.

She sucked in air through her teeth in short bursts, trying to put as little strain as possible on her cracked ribs. She turned her head but then winced in pain at something pulsating in her neck. Right in the middle of the turn she realized that, no matter which move she made, she was going to endure more agony. She pulled herself away from the wall and turned at the waist. Each motion she made looked painful. It took every ounce of courage she had to endure the ordeal. She turned just enough to see Charles. It would have been better had he been in the shadows. The shock wouldn't have been so hard for her had the light not been focused to accent the array of colours on the young boy's face.

Rhoda looked at her son. She tried as hard as a mother can to hold back her tears as she saw the deplorable condition of her boy. Her heart died for him. Her little six-year-old soldier trying so hard to be brave, trying so hard to be the protector in the family. She wanted to comfort him. She wanted to hold him. In a half-sitting, half-lying position, she looked at him, wishing for the strength to be of some use to the only man in her life. But in spite of all the sadness she felt for him, the over-arching emotion that gripped her was guilt. *If only I would have married someone else. If only I could earn money. If only I would be able to keep Daudi happy, none of this would happen. If only. If only. If only.*

With a forced show of courage she stood up in a way that looked like it would break her. She hobbled for a moment, giving the indication she might fall over. Charles looked up at her and wondered if he might not be staring at a reflection of himself. That face. That wretched-looking face. Cuts and blood and swelling and bruises. Charles felt sick to look at her. Rhoda wanted to kiss him, but she knew it would mean pain for both her boy and herself. She reached out her hand, touched him and went outside.

Charles' brothers didn't ask many questions when they woke up. They were still at a young-enough age that a night's sleep was enough to forget the world's problems. They opened the door and looked outside. There, they saw Daudi and Rhoda.

They were seated on the ground. In front of them was a live hen. Daudi was almost in a trance, his eyes focused on nothing in particular. It made Charles uneasy. But he'd seen this before.

"They're praying to the ancestors," Charles told his brothers in a quiet voice, as if to avoid stirring up the sinister spirit from the night before. "They're praying for help. They're praying to be blessed."

Daudi fed the hen milk. He reached for a bowl of *ugali*, a baked dish of crushed maize looking and tasting like a cross between mashed potatoes and cream of wheat, and gave it to the hen. While they didn't have enough food for themselves, they always seemed to have enough food for the hen—their radio for talking to their ancestors.

Yet the more they did this, the poorer they became. Rhoda knew it, but the habit was impossible to break, especially with Daudi. Even at six,

Charles saw how their financial situation grew from bad to worse as they prayed to the hen, hoping that somehow the ancestors would use their powers to change the fortune of the Mulli family and provide food.

There were never prayers for forgiveness. Never prayers of confession about the beatings. There weren't even prayers for Daudi to finally bring home some of the money—any of the money—he made in Nairobi on his trips, instead of drinking it away. Yet there he was, spending what little they had on contacting the ancestors in the hopes of finding a new life.

Daudi and Rhoda stayed there for over an hour. For Charles, it seemed like forever. When it was over, Daudi left their isolated property for the day. The nearest home, Rhoda's mother's, was a ten-minute walk away. Perhaps he had gone to visit her. Or perhaps he had gone the long distance into town to get drunk again. But as much as Charles wanted to be with him, to play with his father like in a normal father-son relationship, he wondered if being without him wasn't the best option for both him and his family.

Rhoda went inside and placed a damp cloth on her ailing face. It looked worse now than before. She lay on her bed the whole day, trying to find that evasive comfortable position. When evening came she was the first to fall asleep. Charles' brothers fell asleep shortly thereafter, while he stayed awake. Listening. Wondering. Hoping. Maybe tonight Dad wouldn't be drunk. Maybe tonight Dad would just come home and go to sleep.

He heard steps coming to the door. They shuffled as they approached, as though someone was losing his balance. He heard a bump. It jolted him. He turned his head away from the door and squeezed his eyes shut, as if doing so would block out the surrounding world.

The door opened. Charles held his breath. Daudi took a step into the hut. *Please. Please. Please. Not tonight. Not again.* Daudi said something. Maybe it was a question. Maybe a curse. Maybe only a grunt. But Charles made no response. He knew better. Daudi repeated himself. Still, Charles held his tongue. There would be no late-night conversations with his father.

Daudi fell down on the bed, rolled over and within moments was sound asleep. Charles listened to his father's heavy breathing, trying to assure himself that Daudi was done for the day. He waited until he was sure they were out of danger. Then he relaxed his tense muscles, closed his eyes and went to sleep.

Had he known what was going to happen the next morning, he wouldn't have been so calm.

It was quiet. That was the first indication of a problem. No sound. Not Daudi. Not Rhoda. Not his brothers. Not even the wind. It was an eerie silence for such a bright, hot day. Charles felt the stillness and wondered what was wrong. He opened his eyes. The swelling had gone down somewhat. It didn't hurt as much to move his jaw. He sat up in his bed.

The hut was empty.

Seeing his mother out of bed was nothing new. She often got up early, especially when she wasn't recovering from a beating, to take care of things on their small farm. Daudi? He could be anywhere. But the brothers were gone. That was another signal to Charles. He normally got up before his brothers. But the bed was empty.

He opened the door. When his eyes adjusted to the light he could make out the mud pathway from the hut to the road. He saw the trees on the property, filled with heavy, green leaves. He saw the dry, black soil of their field off to the right.

But he saw none of his family.

Anxiety gripped him.

He raced out of the house and ran down the path in search of his mother, in search of anyone. Nothing. He ran back and looked behind the hut. Maybe they were playing a game on him. Maybe they were out doing something.

There was no Daudi. That wasn't a concern. For all anyone knew, Daudi had gone into the village for a late-night drink, gotten into a fight and was lying face down in a ditch. But Rhoda and his brothers were gone. That was a problem. That was a very big problem.

He stood in the middle of their property, turning around, hoping to catch a glimpse of someone, anyone. But he saw no one. It was as if they had vanished.

He knew the road to his grandmother's house. With a heart full of fear, he began the lonely and uncertain journey. *Where are they? Where could they have gone? They're at Grandmother's. They'll be there. All of them.*

But when he got closer to his grandmother's house, that hope began to slip away. The brothers weren't playing in the yard. Neither Daudi nor Rhoda was outside. He walked up the path and opened the door. There he found his grandmother, sitting on a small stool, wearing a worried look on her face. She looked up at him. Charles felt sick. He felt certain he was about to get bad news.

"Where are my parents?" he asked, thinking that maybe deep inside he already knew the answer.

His grandmother paused a moment as if to try to hide the information. But the desperate look in Charles' eyes prompted her to tell him what had happened.

"Your family is not here," she said. "They've left you, Charles. They're gone."

CHAPTER 3

"When will they be back?" Charles asked.

"I don't know."

"I'll wait for them."

"Charles."

"We'll wait for them together."

"Charles."

"I'll wait here with you. For Mom and Dad and the brothers to come back. Right? Right? I can wait here with you. Why do you look so sad?"

But reality was starting to creep in on Charles. That look in his grandmother's eyes conveyed everything he needed to know. There was a pain there he had also seen in his mother. He put his hand back on the door as if he wanted to go out, close it, re-enter and hear a different outcome.

"They're coming back soon," he said and waited for his grandmother to respond. But she didn't. "They've gone to Nairobi, haven't they? To look for work. They'll come back. They'll come back tonight."

Still nothing.

He swallowed and took a deep breath. There had to be a simple answer. There had to be a way to find the truth without it being the loss of his family.

"They're moving," he said. "They're getting a house, and then they're coming back to get me."

A tear came to her eye. Even her many years of despair and sadness had not crippled her emotions. She spoke in a gentle, yet convincing, tone to leave no doubt in her young grandson's mind that she was now all that he had.

"No, Charles," she said. "They're gone."

That was the problem with reality. It came in so hard that by the time it was gone it left no room for hope.

"Why?" he asked. "Why would they leave?"

His grandmother pressed her lips together. He was so young, and already he was asking questions for which there were no answers. Why? Why did his parents leave? Why did his father beat them so terribly? Why were they born in poverty while others were born into rich families or in other parts of the world and would never have first-hand knowledge of true lack? Why?

"You will live with me," she said.

But it did little to comfort him.

They both knew she didn't have the means to support him.

Charles stood outside his grandmother's hut. He wore a torn T-shirt and shorts. No shoes. The blistering golden circle above them seemed to occupy every inch of the sky. His forehead was wet with sweat. It was as hot as a sauna.

But the temperature was the least of his worries.

He had gone three days without food, and he wondered how much longer he could go on. He put his hand on his aching stomach. He felt as though a handful of worms were eating him from the inside out—as though someone was sticking a dozen needles into his intestines. The pain was debilitating and constant, unlike any sickness he had ever faced. When a person is ill, there are costly doctors who can help. There is expensive medicine. But the only remedy for hunger is food. And when there is none, there is no cure.

He looked out into the distance, past where his family had lived, towards the next-nearest hut. He stayed there, waiting at his grandmother's hut for hours, trying to find courage. What if they said no? What if other children were around? What if they started laughing? What if they told him he had to bring money? It would be humiliation to an extent he could only imagine.

But the agony in his body demanded restoration regardless of the damage to his pride. Hunger is a cruel lover.

He took a few steps in the direction of the nearest neighbour, just to prove to himself he could do it. He stopped. His pulse shot up, throbbing in his throat. He was really going there. He was really going to do it. Maybe there was another way. Maybe there was something else that could be done. But there wasn't. And he knew it, which is why he was here, getting ready to make the trip any child would dread. He closed his eyes, forced himself to go further and felt the weight of life.

Charles Mulli was going to beg for food.

Every step felt heavy, making it seem as though it was taking much longer than it should to get there. He listened for children playing, hoping they wouldn't be there.

Hoping this would be quick and easy.

But there were children. Running back and forth, playing a game. Some of them he knew. He had played with them at that very same spot. None of them had shoes. None of them could afford it. They had dirty and ripped clothes just like he did. At face value they looked the same as he looked. But they had parents. And they had food. And that was the widest gap a child like Charles had to confront.

When they saw him approaching, they stopped. They knew about Charles. They knew what had happened to him. They hadn't seen him in a few days. One of them called him over to join them. He turned his head away from them, but it did nothing to alleviate his embarrassment. *Just don't look at me. Please don't look at me. Go back to your game and forget that I'm even here.* His wishes, however, went unanswered. They kept looking at him the way children do when they haven't yet learned how painful their innocent gazes can feel. Charles swallowed. Poverty was horrible. No doubt. But lack of privacy about poverty was that much worse.

He felt their stares. It was as if someone had put a pack of wood on his shoulders. If he was coming over to play football, he would have run to them. If he was coming over to join them on a journey to the river, he would have shouted out their names as he approached. But that wasn't the case. Not this time. And now, he was no longer their equal. He was not their companion. He was desperate. He was far, far beneath them. They had food. He had nothing. And it gave them incredible power over him.

He walked past them without answering their greetings. What was he supposed to say? How exactly do you explain to your friends that you are here to beg from their parents? He made it to the hut but felt no relief. The easy part was over. The hard part was about to begin. More sweat poured off of him. It seemed as though the sun had singled him out of all the children in the world and concentrated all of its fire on him alone. The children talked behind him. Why is he here? Why doesn't he say hello? What has he done?

There would be no turning back now. Not after coming this far. He lifted his hand. He curled in his fingers. Time stood still. The children asked more questions.

He knocked on the door.

His pulse slowed down. He felt weak. It was as though he was about to fall down. If he had the strength he would probably have cried. Not that it would have helped. It hadn't helped in the past, and there was no pretending that it would help now. What good were tears?

The door opened. It scared him. There in front of him stood a woman. Her eyes were healthy. Compassionate. Strong. There was expression in her face, unlike the quiet death he was used to seeing hidden behind his mother's eyes. He looked down, ashamed of what he was doing there.

"Charles?" she said.

That was a good sign. She remembered him. Of course she would. He played with her children. It had only been a few days since she last saw him. But that seemed like such a long time ago. And the situation, of course, was much different now.

Charles didn't know what to say. Part of him wished she would have figured out the problem and taken pity on him. How hard was it to realize what was going on here? The other part of him realized that as obvious as his situation was to him, it might not be that obvious to those around him. He couldn't look her in the eye. Not again. There was something about looking a person in the eye that felt as though they could both see right into each other. He had trouble acknowledging his fear and humiliation. He didn't need someone else to see it as well.

Five words. That's it. That's all he had to offer her. Hopefully that's all it would take. But what if she asked questions? How would he respond? What if the children started to laugh? What if *she*, the one with the food, started to laugh? He reached down to a part of him that had never been exposed and opened his soul before her.

"Do you have any food?" he asked.

And at that moment he felt he had died. Actually, dying would have been easier. Anything else would have been easier. It would have been easier to work a fourteen-hour day. It would have been easier to walk to Nairobi. It would have been easier doing tasks normally assigned to boys twice his age.

Anything would have been easier than begging.

And then came the waiting. That was the worst part. How was it possible that while playing football time went by in a flash, yet when standing in front of a woman, pleading for food, an instant seemed like eternity?

"Charles," she said again. This time it felt better. He heard compassion in her voice. It calmed him down. Not that any of it mattered, though. The caring was fine enough. Obviously she could see the need. But it wouldn't make any difference until she got him something to eat.

If, indeed, she would.

He knew he was supposed to look up. That was the polite thing to do, to look someone older than you in the eye. But somehow manners were tougher to practise when pride and self-respect were being destroyed and were now being replaced with a struggle for existence.

She walked away from the door. All he could wonder was whether or not she would return. He heard the children behind him. He felt their stares on his back, piercing him like knives. He wanted to disappear, to turn invisible so as to avoid being the centre of attention for such a thing as this.

She returned. She knelt down to look him in the eye. But he would not look up. He wanted to, but he couldn't. He wanted to say thank you. He wanted to show some kind of appreciation for what she was doing for him. There was food in her hand. His eyes grew wider. He swallowed. A small package with enough for two days. Two days. Two whole days of food. That meant a night of going to sleep without wondering if there would be food the next day. At least one night he could go to bed with the certainty that there would be something to eat when he awoke. But he said nothing and made no eye contact. She placed the package with both of her hands into his hand, touching his arm in the process. His eyes suddenly stung with pain. He closed them a moment to keep the tears from progressing any further. The touch of a woman. The touch of a mother. *Just a hug. That's it. Please can I have just one hug? Just for a moment. Even if the kids laugh, I don't care now. Not any more. I just need to know that I'm still the kind of kid a mother would want. I need to know that I'm loved. Am I?*

He turned and left. She called his name, but he kept walking, right past the children who stood watching, not knowing whether to greet him or continue with their game. He wiped the tears from his eyes and felt the weight of the food in his hands. Tonight there was food.

Tonight there was food.

For two years, Charles begged around his home. Many times people opened the doors only to close them when they saw the beggar at the door. Sometimes a person gets accustomed to pain. But Charles never developed immunity to rejection. Each day he would make the painful journey from hut to hut until someone would take pity on him. Sometimes it was done out of love. Sometimes it was done just to get rid of him, just to have him out of their presence, out of their minds and out of the way.

But one evening hope came when a child from the village came running up to him. Charles sat on a rock, unaware of his approaching friend, looking out at the quiet African evening. The burning sun set behind the hills taking with it the relentless heat. Tomorrow it would rise and set again. Then the day after and the day after. And it occurred to him that the search for food would go on tomorrow as it had every day. And it would go on and on and on, and it made him wonder what on earth the point of all this was.

Charles heard approaching steps. He turned around. The child stopped in front of him, out of breath. "She's here!"

"Who?" Charles asked.

"Your mother. She's back. She's back, Charles!"

Charles stood up. The depressing thoughts about life being an endless cycle left him. The sun may have been setting, but for him it was high noon. Mom was back. The touch of his mother. He ran to the road as fast as he could.

His calloused bare feet raced over the rocky path. His heart pounded in his chest. His eyes scanned the horizon looking for his mother.

Life had come back.

He made the turn to his grandmother's hut. He saw some of the uncles standing outside. As he hurried past them one of them tried to grab him. But he avoided him, thinking nothing of it.

Charles came into the hut with a burst of energy that shocked everyone inside. His eyes were wide in anticipation, his breathing heavy from all the running. He scanned the room. And what he saw made his heart stop.

There was a woman there. She sat beside his grandmother. But it wasn't his mother. Couldn't be. He stared at her in disbelief.

The woman in front of him was unrecognizable. Her head was so swollen that it looked like a massive balloon. Cuts. Bruises. Swelling. Her eyes were shut. She tilted her head back in order to see what she could out of one eye that let in a sliver of light. The sides of her head had thick marks on them, looking like wounds coming from a piece of metal.

Her arms were puffy. There were lumps all over her. Charles felt a glob in his throat, as if he was about to vomit.

No one said anything. The quiet reminded him of the nights he stayed awake in his bed waiting for his father to come home and beat them.

Charles cried a helpless cry, the kind only an abandoned child without food or a future cries when the little they have in life is ruined in front of their eyes.

Grandmother cried, too. But Mother didn't. Somehow her tears didn't work when her face was that mangled.

He tried not to look. As much as he wanted to be in constant eye contact with her, his spirit couldn't allow it. He was angry. He was bitter at his father. She couldn't fight back. She couldn't defend herself. He wished, he wished so much that he were bigger. Then he could give it back to his father. If he were taller and tougher he could walk into his father's hut with a bat or a shovel and ruin his father the way his father had ruined her. No more problems. No remorse. He clenched his jaw, and at eight years old he hated everything about his life.

"Wakya," she said (*pronounced wa-cha*), which means "Hello, how are you?"

But Charles had nothing to say. Pain. Anger. Remorse. Revenge. A collision of emotions burned through him, making it impossible to decide which one to choose. But in the end, the pain won out. His poor mother. Tears ran down his cheeks as he felt the helplessness that comes with not being able to make right what is terribly wrong.

But there was more.

Off to the side was a new baby, Zachariah. Charles looked closer. Something was not right. The child was sick. Or worse. He stepped closer and saw marks on the baby. Grandmother explained what had happened. As a mother instinctively would, Rhoda had tried to protect the baby during the fight with Daudi. She used her body as a shield between the baby and the punishing blows from Daudi, who, with a closed fist, pummelled down on Rhoda's head. Fist after fist smashed into her as she struggled to run away from Daudi with her baby to find a place of refuge. But, as in every beating she had suffered, she was unable to get away from Daudi. She tried to hang on as long as she could, but the blows to the head made it impossible for her to concentrate. The baby slipped out of her hands and fell into the fire, burning his head and hands.

Whatever joy Charles could have had in seeing his new brother was destroyed by the suffering this infant was already having to go through.

That night, Uncle Nzyoka took Rhoda and the baby to the hospital. When Charles lay down on his bed, his mind was filled with agony and uncertainty about his mother and brother. That image of his mother with the horrifying marks and swelled head haunted him. She'd been through beatings before. Many of them. But this was the worst. And with it came the realization that he might never see her or his young brother again.

CHAPTER 4

Charles lived the next days with the anxiety of knowing a messenger might come to their hut at any moment to tell them his mother and brother were dead. Every time a person walked by, every time he played with the other children, every time he begged for food, he knew he was never more than a step away from hearing the bad news.

But it never came. Instead, Rhoda returned with Zachariah. A friend told Charles they were back. He ran to the hut with less expectation than he had the last time. He opened the door and hoped this encounter wouldn't be a repeat of what he saw the last time. It wasn't. He felt relieved to have at least a moment of certainty in life. He made eye contact with his mother. He recognized her. She had been healed.

On the outside, anyway.

He gave his mother a hug. As he felt her arms around him, he realized in an instant what he had been missing all this time. They stayed there in the silence, not saying anything. Not needing to. She was back, and they were together. For how long, he didn't know. But he'd already learned the non-existence of permanence and instead allowed himself to be a boy with a mother for the moment.

He sat down on a stool next to his baby brother. Zachariah's brown eyes were so big that Charles could make out a partial reflection of himself in them. He touched his fingers and saw the healing burn marks.

Weeks later it was Daudi's turn to come back. News came to Charles as he was eating the ugali a neighbour had given them. "Your father is coming." Those words went like daggers through his ears and into his heart. Instead of feeling the joy a child should have in seeing his father, Charles felt a paralyzing fear. *Why is he here? What does he want? What is he going to do to us?*

Daudi was at the peak of his fatherhood when he was absent.

Charles saw him coming down the path to Grandmother's. Strange how that small man appeared so terribly tall. Even under the hot sun, Daudi's face looked cold, causing a chill to run down Charles' back. He glanced at Charles as he walked into the hut for a meeting with the relatives. No smile. No hug. No words.

What was there to say?

While Charles waited outside, Daudi was inside making promises he couldn't keep...*I won't beat her. I won't drink. I will provide. I will look after the kids* and on and on and on. They lived in a time when there was no government to appeal to. No formal justice department. No police force. No shelters. The only recourse in spousal abuse was the tribal council. And when the tribal council got involved, things got very serious. It was the last resort people used, because of the severity of the consequences. If they were called into the matter, there would be no middle road. Guilty or innocent. That was it. If found innocent, he would go free. If found guilty, he would be strapped face down to the ground with ropes and whipped with heavy sticks until his back split open, leaving him either paralyzed or, more likely, dead. Thinking back on the meeting later, Charles figured his dad wasn't there to be an honest husband or responsible father or to carry out his promises, but rather to appease his in-laws so as not to bring the death sentence from the tribal council upon himself.

At least for now.

It wasn't until years later that Charles learned the real reason why his family had left. Rhoda's brothers kicked her and Daudi off the property, forcing Daudi to look for his own land. Rhoda had chickens that ruined her brothers' neighbouring coffee plants, causing unrest. According to African culture, daughters do not inherit anything. So in the minds of her brothers the property she inhabited really belonged to them. She was living there on borrowed time. The brothers had enough of her and booted her and Daudi out. Daudi and Rhoda left Charles there because he was in grade one and they didn't want to interrupt his studies. But even a bad goodbye would have been better than no goodbye.

Daudi emerged from the meeting with Rhoda and Zacharias looking neither happy nor sad. He took his family (including Charles, this
time) and moved out of Kathithyamaa.

They went by bus to Nairobi on their way to a place called Mollo in
the Rift Valley, where Daudi and the other boys worked as labourers on
a farm owned by a man named Kavulu. It was a long bus ride, especially
for Charles. His father was sober during that trip. It was at times like
these when he wasn't transformed into tangible evil by alcohol that he
actually seemed human to Charles. He talked to Rhoda on the way there.
    But very little to Charles.
    After arriving in Nairobi, they took another bus to Mollo. The
whole way there Charles did what he could to forget his childhood.
Perhaps he could leave his memories in Kathithyamaa and start over.
Perhaps the new location would mark the beginning of a whole new life
for all of them. With every passing kilometre Charles hoped the past
would be forgotten—being too young, of course, to realize that distance
plays no role in overcoming the problems from earlier experiences in life.
    They walked eleven kilometres from the bus stop in Mollo to
Kavulu's farm. When they got there, Charles looked out over the vast
array of short, white pyrethrum flowers, which were used to make
insecticide. They looked like a massive white blanket covering the
earth all the way to the horizon. He turned to his right and saw hundreds of cows. He had never seen so many. Acre after acre of animals
and white flowers spread for what seemed like forever. Small huts dotted the landscape here and there as far as he could see. He looked in
all directions, soaking in the expanse and wondering how it was that
one man came to own all this. How do people get so wealthy? Was he
always this rich? Could somebody really start with nothing and
become as rich as this?
    He saw three boys working together off in the distance. They were
crouched over, digging around the plants. One of the boys looked up to
wipe sweat from his forehead.
    Charles took his attention off the three boys, not expecting them to
be the ones for whom he was looking. But when he looked back, he
thought he recognized them. He looked closer. It was them. He walked
in their direction and then broke into a run, calling out to his brothers.
They looked over and saw him. Dropping their shabby hand tools, they
stood up as Charles hugged them and shook their hands. They were thin.

Too thin. Their eyes were sunken. Daudi came, as did Rhoda carrying Zacharias. And there they were. Together for the first time as a family.

The hut where Daudi, Rhoda and the three brothers stayed was small, so Charles went to live down the road with his paternal grandfather, Kaleli. He hadn't seen him in years and felt nervous about what seeing him would be like. He walked up to the hut, wondering whether his grandfather was like his father. A medium-sized man with a strong build came out to meet him. He had a smile on his face. Charles felt a genuineness in him he hadn't seen in his father.

"Hello, Charles. I'm glad you're here," Kaleli said in a way Daudi never had.

Instead of shyness, Charles felt welcomed. Instead of fear, Charles felt loved.

Charles reached out to shake his hand, but instead Kaleli bent down and gave him a hug to welcome him to his new home.

They settled his things, what little he had, and then Kaleli sat down outside on wood stumps with Charles and talked about stories from Africa. Kaleli had such passion, such interest in sharing his life with Charles, that, at first, Charles felt overwhelmed. *Why is he talking to me? Why is he so interested in telling me these stories? Doesn't he have other things to do besides spend time with me?* The two of them often talked until bedtime about his school, Kaleli's work, Africa and anything that was on their minds.

Perhaps this is what a father could be like.

It was another afternoon of studying. Kaleli was out at work, leaving Charles at home by himself to do his schoolwork and chores. Kaleli had a shaving knife that caught Charles' interest. He switched his attention back and forth between the knife and his studies and wondered if it would work well for whittling a stick. He got up to get a closer look at the knife. The steel blade was sharp. He saw his reflection in it. He touched it. The blade felt cool under his skin. *Just for a few minutes. Nobody will notice. Just to see what it feels like in my hand.*

He took the knife and sat down on his upside-down pail that he used as a chair. He grabbed a nearby stick in his left hand and began to carve. The knife cut well. Smooth and effortless. He felt it glide down with each stroke as he stripped the bark off the branch making a sharp point. He was about to turn the stick over to continue on the other side when the knife suddenly slipped. It veered off at an awkward angle. It sliced into his thumb.

The shock of what happened raced through Charles. He tried to calm himself down. It didn't look bad. Not at first. But when the blood began spurting out, he felt light-headed and thought he would throw up. He reached for a nearby rag and wrapped it around his hand, hoping to stop the bleeding.

He cleaned the knife as best he could and put it back. His throbbing hand ached. He sat down and tried to regulate his breathing. It helped to keep him calm, but the pain continued. Part of him wanted to see if it was as bad as he thought it was. The other part wanted to keep the rag on so as not to thwart any healing that was already taking place.

Kaleli would be coming home soon. It scared Charles. He had to clear his tracks. So he made the fire as he always did and hurried out into the bush to hide.

Kaleli came home and called for Charles. But Charles did not respond. He sat out in the bushes looking at his grandfather, trying to figure out what kind of mood he was in. It was cold outside. He shivered. But the cold was better than a beating. Charles would know. He waited for hours. It got dark. His body shook uncontrollably. He was hungry. He was tired. He was in pain. Maybe Kaleli was asleep by now. Maybe he could sneak inside and get into bed without Kaleli noticing and by tomorrow all would be forgotten. He waited a few more minutes, listening for any hint of movement in the hut. Not hearing anything, he decided to chance it.

Charles hurried towards the hut. He stopped outside and waited to see if he could hear Grandfather inside. Nothing. He opened the door hoping not to make a sound. He stepped inside. There was Kaleli.

Awake.

Waiting for him.

Charles closed the door and avoided looking at Kaleli. He sat down on his pail. He hid his hand behind him as best he could without looking obvious.

"Where have you been?" Kaleli asked.

No response.

"Charles?" Kaleli said.

Kaleli had seen the blood on the knife. But even if he hadn't, Charles' suspicious silence was enough.

"Yes?" Charles said, hoping that by stalling he could figure out an excuse.

"I've been worried about you. Where have you been?"

Charles looked down at the ground. "I used your knife. I wasn't sup-posed to," Charles said, knowing that at any moment a terrifying hand would strike him across the face, sending him sprawling to the ground.

"What happened?"

"I used it to cut a stick. The knife slipped." He pulled out his hand from behind his back, thinking this to be the least of the injuries he would suffer once Kaleli dished out the punishment. "I cut myself."

Kaleli took the rag off Charles' hand and inspected the wound. The cut was deep.

"Who gave you permission?" Kaleli asked.

"No one."

The beating was coming. That much he knew. That much was cer-tain. That's what men did, all men, when their sons or grandsons did something wrong. His father hit him for the slightest infraction. Using a knife without permission would definitely be included in the list of rea-sons for a beating that would leave lifelong marks.

He did not look into Kaleli's eyes. That would only make things worse. He tightened his shoulders, waiting for the first strike to come.

But he was about to receive something else.

CHAPTER 5

Kaleli wasn't nearly as strong as Daudi. A hit from him wouldn't hurt as bad as one from his father. But he worried that maybe he had underestimated his grandfather and that, perhaps, Kaleli had what it took to inflict real damage. Charles kept a careful watch on Kaleli's hands to see which direction the first strike would come from.

But it never came.

"Your hand. Does it hurt?"

There was something in the tone of his voice. There was something in the way he asked that question that felt altogether different for Charles.

"No," Charles said.

"The cut does not look very bad. You are going to be all right."

Charles nodded his head. *Why isn't he striking out at me? Why is he talking to me?*

"Knives are dangerous. Wouldn't you agree?" Kaleli said with a smile.

Charles caught a glimpse of his grandfather. He looked at his hands. They stood still at his sides.

"They are," Charles said.

"You must be hungry? And cold, I presume," Kaleli said, adding a short laugh.

The room felt different. Even though it was late at night, it seemed Kaleli's response brought light into the hut. Charles relaxed his shoulders. They hurt from being tensed while bracing for the beating.

"I am."

"Well?"

Charles gathered his courage and looked his grandfather in the eye. He saw no anger. He saw no violence. He saw no indication that a fit of rage was about to be released. Instead, he saw something compelling. Kaleli's eyes looked different than what he had gotten used to seeing in his father's eyes.

"Well…?" Charles replied, not sure where Kaleli was going with this.

"You'll need some supper before you go to bed. Sit down."

Charles sat down on his pail. Kaleli put some of the daily meal of cabbage and ugali in a bowl for Charles. He sat down across from him.

"And Charles?"

"Yes."

"Don't repeat that any more without my permission. I don't want you to get hurt."

I don't want you to get hurt. As Charles began eating, those words went over and over in his mind. A meal instead of a beating. Compassion instead of aggression. Conversation instead of a one-way screaming match.

Kaleli told more stories of Africa. He talked about what it was like to grow up in this country and the changes that had taken place. When they were finished eating, Kaleli washed Charles' wound and wrapped a piece of cloth around it. Already it showed signs of healing. Charles went to bed thinking about what his grandfather had just done for him.

I don't want you to get hurt.

The family spent three months in Mollo. Life was as normal as a child like Charles could expect it to be. His family had work. He had school. He lived in security, without fear of harm, with his grandfather. His only real worry was for his mother. Rhoda had a sense of loyalty to Daudi. Why? Charles did not know. She lived under Daudi, a brutal dictator who treated her worse than a slave. But she stuck with him, both out of a sense of duty and out of a horrible fear of knowing she'd be severely beaten if she ever tried to leave. He had hoped that Daudi would have changed his ways now that he had steady work. But he hadn't and the ongoing threat of abuse hung over Rhoda's head like thunderclouds that show signs of an imminent storm.

Charles woke up on a cloudy morning and put on his uniform of khaki shorts, a grey shirt and a green cardigan. He left for school while his father and grandfather went to work in the fields. It started like any other normal day.

But it would not end that way.

When he came home from school, he stopped by his parents' hut. None of his brothers played outside. He went inside. His mother wasn't there. Neither were any of their family's belongings.

The place had been deserted.

A shot of fear pounded through him. He tried to control his panic. *They haven't left. They're out somewhere. They've moved to a larger hut for all of us. There wasn't enough room in this one. They've found a better place so that all of us can live together.*

He went to his grandfather's hut, sat down on his pail and wondered what was going on.

When Kaleli came home in the evening, he opened the door and looked into the eyes of a child who was wondering whether he was revisiting his fate of abandonment. Charles didn't have to ask. Kaleli's expression told him the truth.

He closed the door behind him and sat down on his wooden chair. They waited together in silence, Charles dreading to hear the words he knew were about to come.

"They've gone to Nakuru," Kaleli said.

"All of them?"

"Yes, all of them."

"Where are they staying?"

"I don't know. They don't know either. They're hoping to find a place."

"When are they coming back?"

That was a bad question. Kaleli was wise and knew not to answer.

There was no point in crying. There was no point in wishing things weren't the way they were. Charles had already learned the futility of getting angry at a situation for which there was no remedy.

"So they're gone?" Charles asked, having developed a certain callousness from the rejections he had already faced.

"They're gone."

"Then there's nothing left to say, is there?" He took in a breath. The tears would come later. "I'll start the fire for supper."

The days felt long to Charles. School was a disaster. He worked extremely hard and was among the top in his class. But school, of course, is much more than just grades. The trouble came with the children around him. He had very few friends at a time when he could have really used them. During breaks and after school, the children would yell at Charles because he was an orphan. "*Bure! Bure!*" they would yell at him, which means "You are nothing!" Over and over again he heard that word and dozens like it. While it hurt him to hear it, the children's reaction to him made perfect sense. If his own parents, his own flesh and blood, rejected him, why then would strangers want anything to do with him?

Some evenings he would come home and cry in his bed. He wanted to tell his mother what had happened. He wanted to hear her reassuring words of affirmation. He wanted to feel her arms around him. He wanted to know he was loved in spite of the comments from all those around him. But there was no mother.

Not for Charles.

Sometimes Kaleli would come home drunk, but not violent, and Charles, at the age of ten, would have to cook for himself. Cabbage, ugali, water and sometimes a tea called *chai*. No bread. No meat. He learned to get water, make a fire and become self-reliant.

Charles stood with his only friend, Khamisi, on a field overlooking a herd of sheep. The sun was getting ready to set. It was a warm evening. That day had been particularly difficult for Charles. The schoolchildren had been especially vicious. It was the end of the week, and the cruelty of his classmates, the loss of his family and the drunkenness of his grandfather weighed more heavily on him than in previous weeks. Because Khamisi was about his age and looked after sheep, the two of them would sometimes come to the field to play games and talk.

"I'm sorry things aren't going well for you, my friend," Khamisi said.

Charles shrugged his shoulders. He didn't want to talk about a problem for which there was no solution.

"I'm an orphan. What should I be expecting?"

"Well, if it makes any difference, you are not alone. They say Africa is full of orphans just like you. Even right here in Kenya."

"How many do you suppose there are?"

"Like the grass in the field, I'm told. They say there are parents who leave their children and abandon them to the streets. Especially in the big cities. They can't afford them, so the children take off in the hopes of finding something to eat. Even the children in the slums who have parents aren't much better off. There are terrible stories about what some parents force their daughters to do."

"Meaning?"

Khamisi became quiet. He shot a nervous glance to his friend and then looked back into the distance. "It's terrible. The girls. They force them to…to do things with men so that they can bring in money for the family. The boys. They steal; they threaten people. They become animals, struggling to survive. Even these sheep have it better than they do."

Charles nodded his head. Thinking about those orphans, those thousands of unwanted or degraded children, made him sick.

Khamisi dug a small hole in the ground. The two of them took a few steps back and took turns throwing Khamisi's small coin into the hole to see who could get closer.

"Who helps them?" Charles asked.

"The children?"

"Yes. The boys on the street. The girls. Who is there to help them?"

"The same people who are helping you, I suppose."

It was raining when Charles got back to the hut. He was tired, inside and out. All he wanted was to have supper, go to sleep and forget the week's troubles. But when he came inside, he saw Kaleli sitting at the table with an expression on his face that told him the week was not yet done.

"Charles, sit down."

He hadn't done anything wrong. Hadn't taken the knife. Hadn't neglected his chores. This conversation was not going to be about a reprimand. Charles sat down on his pail. He felt uncertain and wondered why Kaleli wanted to have a talk.

"What is it?" Charles asked, not wanting to know the answer.

Kaleli hesitated, and it only confirmed Charles' suspicion that what he was about to hear was going to be difficult.

Kaleli swallowed. Even though he'd rehearsed this many times, it somehow seemed much more difficult when it came right down to it. He knew there would be no easy way to deliver the news. He looked Charles in the eye and said it slowly so that he would not have to repeat it.

"I can no longer care for you," he said.

This time there were no daggers in Charles' heart. There was no panic in his spirit. No tears about to well up in his eyes. He'd been here before. He knew the drill.

"Where do I go?" he asked.

"You'll need to go to your parents."

"My parents don't want me."

"They'll have to."

"Grandfather. They don't want me."

"They will have to take you, Charles."

"They won't."

"They will. They have to."

Charles said nothing. There was no point in arguing. He'd already learned that once someone has made up their mind about refusing to help there is little that can be done to change it.

"Charles, I have no money. I cannot support you. I want to, but you have to understand I do not have the means."

"I do not know where they live."

"They are in Nakuru."

"I have never been there. I have no address. How will I find them in such a big town?"

"You will find a way."

"I don't know anyone there. How will I find a way?"

Kaleli had no idea. He only knew that Charles had to go to his parents. How he would find them was anybody's guess.

"I will give you the money for the train."

"And then?"

"Then you will find your parents."

"And if I can't? What if I can't find them?"

"You will. You have to."

"What if they've moved on? What if they are no longer there? What if they refuse to let me come into their home? What if—"

He stopped himself. This was pointless. Tomorrow he would be on his way to Nakuru, regardless of whether these questions were answered or not.

He nodded his head, giving Kaleli the indication that he didn't like the result but he understood it was time to go. He put on a confident look that was much too mature for a boy his age and thanked Kaleli for taking him in for as long as he had. He thanked him for all their excellent conversations about Africa. He would remember those his entire life. But as he went to sleep that night, he was most thankful that his grandfather had never beaten him. There was something very reassuring about living in that kind of safety.

The next morning he said goodbye to his only friend, Khamisi. Kaleli took him to the station, where they said their farewells. It didn't feel like he was leaving. It seemed as though he was just going away for a day and coming back in the evening to talk about Africa with his grandfather again.

He got on board the hot train and sat next to a window. People crowded in, filling seats all around him. A horn blew. The train jerked forward. The buildings began to move backwards. And as the train pulled down the track, he saw the last images of his grandfather, waving among the people disappearing in the distance. He wondered if he would ever see him again. He wondered what Nakuru had in store. But mostly, he wondered if the father who had abandoned him would take him back in this, his most desperate hour.

CHAPTER 6

Everything looked different.

Charles stared out the train window in amazement. There were many, many more people here in Nakuru than he had ever seen in his entire life. There were cars everywhere. People lined the streets, selling corn, drinks, newspapers, shoes—all sorts of things. It was busy. People pushing past each other, trying to cross the street, buying this or selling that. It was loud. Honking horns. People shouting. Hammering from a construction site. Being on the train while it was travelling gave Charles a sense of refuge. But the moment the train began slowing down on its approach into Nakuru, he felt a tug in his chest. At first he thought it might be another stop on the way into town. But when he heard people behind him remark that this was Nakuru, he realized the journey was over.

It was time to begin the search.

He turned away from the window. He had a small bag with him that he had kept on his lap the whole trip. He stood up and moved over to the aisle. People walked past him. He waited until everyone was off and then walked the aisle to the door by himself. He took the steps down to the ground and walked off the train. It was official. Charles Mulli was alone in a strange town.

Where to begin? He walked down the platform and spotted a group of people talking together. They were well dressed—at least better than he was. When he came up to them, they looked at him as though he was about to begin begging them for money.

"Do you know where Daudi and Rhoda Mulli live?" he asked. All the years he spent begging for food made it easier to ask for help in finding his parents.

"No," one of them replied.

"Do you know someone who might know?"

"We can't help you. I'm sorry."

If they really were sorry, they didn't show it. They turned back to their conversation.

Charles walked further down the road. For a city with so many people it seemed unusually clean. No garbage on the streets. No people, besides Charles, begging for help.

"Excuse me," he said to an elderly man who wouldn't slow down. "Sir, excuse me." The man turned and looked at Charles. "Sir, would you—"

But that was enough for the man. He wanted no more and kept walking.

Through the streets, person by person, business by business, Charles approached people, asking for help. Most responded to him. None could help. By evening he had talked to more people in five hours than he had in his entire life—all without any success. He had no money for food, and the few provisions he brought on the train had long since been eaten. People in hotels saw him walking the streets by himself, and some offered him something to eat. He asked them for help in finding his parents, but while they wanted to offer assistance there was no one who knew where the Mullis could be found.

He returned to the train station late that night. The shelter had a corrugated metal roof. He lay down in the corner on the cold concrete and tried as best he could to fall asleep in this new city. He wondered if his parents had moved on and how he would track them down if they had. Tomorrow would be another day. Hopefully there would be food. And hopefully he would find his parents.

But the second day proved to be much the same as the first. A few people gave him something to eat and wished him well in his search. But wishes did little to help him. Over and over again he approached people.

"Excuse me, can you help me?"

"Would you happen to know where I can find the Mullis?"

"Have you ever heard of Daudi or Rhoda Mulli?"

"I have nothing to eat and no place to sleep. Can you help me?"

When he went to sleep the second night, he had more doubts about ever finding his parents. Hope was crashing into reality, and it occurred to him that he had reached the end. He needed someone to help him. Someone who could take him to his parents. The world truly was a merciless place. It was as cold as concrete.

And in all his searches, in all his troubles, the thought of God never entered his mind.

The next day someone took him to the police to see if they could help. He sat down on a wooden chair as a man dressed in a uniform came to him.

"You are looking for your parents?" he asked.

Charles nodded. "I was told they are here." He gave their names.

The officer gave him a cup of tea and some bread and told him they would look for them. Five hours later the officer returned. "We have found their house," he said. "Come, I will take you there."

When the officer brought him to the house, Charles did not know whether to feel relieved or anxious. The first part of his journey was over. He had made it to his parents' home again. But now came the real question.

"Here it is," the officer said.

"Thank you," Charles said, wondering what kind of reception he would get.

He walked up to the small house. He turned around and saw the officer leave. Charles knocked on the door. There was no response. He knocked again and waited. The door opened. He hoped it wouldn't be Daudi. It wasn't.

It was his mother.

She looked at him with amazement. Her mouth dropped open. She got down on her knees and wrapped her arms around Charles. She began to cry. It had been five months since they had seen each other, and it showed in the way she grasped him. There was desperation in her embrace, as though she couldn't bear to let him go again. "How was the train ride? Are you all right? How did you find us?" He answered her questions and felt the compassion that comes with being able to look a long-lost mother in the eye.

His brothers ran to the house and shouted when they saw him. They laughed as they hugged each other. He told them about Mollo and they told him about Nakuru as they ate a meal together. The one-room house had no electricity, so when the sun set they had to use oil lamps to see each other. There they stayed in the shadows, talking with each other until late in the evening.

As Charles lay down to sleep for the evening, he wondered what his mother really thought about him coming back. He was another mouth to feed. Another burden. If they really wanted him, if they really loved him, they would have told him they were leaving. And not just once. It had happened twice. So far. What kind of parent leaves a child behind? It wasn't a mistake. That much he knew. They intentionally left him behind. And as he lay on the floor with a thin blanket over him, he felt awkward and embarrassed, realizing he was unwanted but having no other recourse but to live with the very parents who wanted nothing to do with him.

It was near midnight when Daudi came home. They were all asleep, including Charles, who was exhausted after all his adventures and an afternoon of playing football with his brothers. Daudi was drunk, again. He opened the door to their shabby house. As if warned by his presence, Charles woke up and saw his father.

"Why are you here?" Daudi asked, implying he was neither angry nor excited to see Charles. "You're supposed to be in school."

Charles explained that Grandpa Kaleli sent him here.

"What?" Daudi said, with his voice becoming more intense. It scared Charles, making him think he'd just said enough to set Daudi off. "Why did he send you here? Why doesn't he take the responsibility of looking after you?"

Charles wasn't quite sure what to say to his father about Kaleli's apparent irresponsibility in taking care of him. He said nothing.

Daudi didn't get violent. Not this time. He closed the door. Charles heard him stumble down the hallway, bang into a wall and collapse into bed.

School fees proved to be too expensive in Nakuru compared with rural settings. After only a few months with his family, Daudi shipped Charles off to school back in Kathithyamaa in Machakos district to again live with his grandmother on his mother's side.

He said goodbye to his mother and brothers. Again. His mother cried. Again. The reality of finances forced Charles back onto that train. As it started down the tracks, his mother waved. He waved back until she was out of sight. He sat back in his seat. Alone. Again.

The uncles weren't happy about having Charles staying on the property, *their* property. They felt there was some ulterior reason for him being there—that, perhaps, being blood related, he was laying claim to that piece of land. So they told him he was not welcome to live with them and forced him to move down the road, about a kilometre away, with his Aunt Muthikwa.

"Hello," Charles said when he saw her. He felt like a piece of scrap metal being thrown around to whomever can make use of it. Or tolerate it. He was prepared to be pushed on to someplace else. But he was running out of relatives.

"Welcome, Charles," she said. Everything about her—the look in her eyes, the tone of her voice, her smile—convinced him she meant it.

She took him into her small home, made him a little bed and sat him down to give him some ugali. She talked with him about his life and about his schooling. There was a genuine warmth about her that convinced Charles she wanted him. Yes, she was a relative. There was at least some part of her that had to take him in. But the others hadn't paid attention to that inherent responsibility, and she was now doing more than just her duty. He felt she was taking an interest in him.

And he hoped it would last.

Her husband, Masyuko, however, was not happy about the arrangement.

"Why is he staying here?" he shouted when he found out the news. He was drunk (a family tradition). It was late.

"He has no place else to go," Muthikwa replied.

"So what? I don't want this boy here!"

"He's our relative."

"He's a waste!"

"We owe him this. We need to help him."

"We owe him nothing!"

Masyuko was tall. He towered over her like a giant. She pleaded with him to let Charles stay, hoping his shouting would not wake him. She didn't want Charles to hear what his uncle thought of him. But Charles was awake, only pretending to be asleep. He knew about drunken men. It was better they assumed he was not listening.

"Please let him stay," she said.

"It's not my fault his father can't take care of him!"

"He has no place else to go." She began to cry. She held the tears back as best she could, but hearing her husband talk about their young nephew this way made it impossible for her to control herself.

"I don't want the boy here, and that's final!"

But Muthikwa opposed the decision. So she woke Charles, got him out of bed, and the two slept outside.

Each day when Charles came home from school, Muthikwa had food ready for him and listened to his stories. They talked about Africa. She helped him with his homework. She taught him how to cook.

"I love you," she said to him.

He tried to remember the last time he had heard those words. It wasn't very common to hear them in African culture. But when someone said them, it was understood they really meant them. He looked into her eyes and saw a woman of compassion. She had volunteered to sleep outside with him and take care of him, even though she would have been much better off had she turned him away.

"Why?" Charles asked. "Why do you love me?"

Muthikwa laughed. Some women can set the whole world right with the tone of their laughter. Muthikwa was one of them.

"Do I need a reason?"

Charles looked into her eyes. What had he done to deserve this from her? He wasn't bringing in money. He wasn't bringing in anything. He was costing them food. Why would she love him?

Masyuko never took to Charles. The verbal abuse continued and got worse as time went on. "You are nobody's son!" he yelled at him over and over again. And finally, Charles had had enough.

This time he sent himself away.

Saying goodbye to Muthikwa, who had become a mother to him, was difficult. He never did say goodbye to Masyuko.

Charles went to neighbouring towns to work as a labourer. He dug holes for coffee and maize plants and picked coffee beans. He paid for his own schooling fees and found shelter in a number of homes with people who would take him in. But all the moving around did little to help him advance in school. Years before, when he was seven, he started grade one. Now that he was eleven, he was still in grade one.

Unable to get a place in regular school, he had to go to evening classes, where he spent two hours a day learning after a long day of work. He became the class monitor while he was in grades one, two and three. After earning enough money from his work, he was able to go to school during the day. When he was fourteen years old and in grade four, the teachers and students in grades one to six voted for Charles to become the prefect of the school. He became responsible for overseeing the conduct of the children, seeing to it that all the children were in class and ensuring only English was spoken, no Swahili or dialect.

When he wasn't working, going to school or studying, Charles sometimes lay awake at night thinking about his life. He wondered about his parents and about being sent from place to place. He had rarely been any place where he was truly wanted. Usually he ended up in places where he was only tolerated. *What did I do to deserve this? Why didn't I get proper love and care? Why have people, especially my parents, been so cruel to me?* He didn't get the answers to those questions.

Not then.

It was May 1965 when a friend invited sixteen-year-old Charles to a church youth rally in Kathithyamaa. He'd heard of the African Brotherhood Church but had no idea what it was about or why his friend wanted him to come. When they got to the church, he saw three hundred young people, about fifteen to twenty-two years old, gathered in anticipation. When he stepped onto the property, he felt something strange. There was something different in the air. Something unseen. For a moment he felt the horror he had encountered when his father had come home drunk to beat him and his mother. But then he felt something much stronger. Something non-threatening. There was a power there he had never felt before.

They found seats in the middle near the aisle. A group at the front led them in a number of songs that Charles had never heard before. When they sat down, a middle-aged preacher in a black suit and tie spoke to them in a quiet voice that managed to carry over the entire group.

Charles had never met the man before, never even seen him before, and yet, as he spoke about Jesus coming down to die on the cross for everyone's sins and the need for forgiveness Charles had the unmistakable feeling that the preacher was speaking directly to him.

"He loves you," the preacher said.

It was as though all 300 people had vanished and only Charles and the preacher remained.

"You must surrender your life to Jesus Christ in order to have salvation."

Someone besides the preacher was speaking to Charles. For the first time in his life, he heard a voice around him, inside him, telling him that this was the moment when he needed to respond to God—to a friend who would stick close to him, unlike the many people who had abandoned him in his life.

"If you want to receive Jesus," the preacher said, "I want you to raise your hand."

Charles was so sure, so confident, that his hand shot up.

"Take a step of faith and come to the front."

Charles walked without fear. He had never known such courage before. He came to the front with others. The electricity was palpable. It felt as though there would be a tremendous explosion.

"If you want to receive Jesus Christ as your personal Saviour, then I encourage you to repeat these lines after me," the preacher said.

"God, I need You. You love me. Thank You, Jesus, for dying on the cross. I ask You to forgive my sins. I give You my life, and I ask You to make me Your child and to follow You."

That was it. Short. To the point. Sincere. When Charles finished praying, he felt the greatest relief, as though he was finally able to breathe as never before. Suddenly there was an alternative to the bitterness he had towards his family and his life's circumstances. He wasn't some piece of trash. He wasn't some worthless orphan without a future. He wasn't just another face in the crowd. He was valuable. He was part of a family.

He was loved.

And at that moment, Charles knew that God was his friend.

CHAPTER 7

Charles left the crusade feeling the effects of what had just happened. He sensed a charge inside him that gave him such energy it almost felt unnatural. It was unlike anything he had ever encountered before. There was power. Somewhere inside him there was a definite power that seemed altogether stronger than the demonic forces that had attacked him and his father. And although he didn't know it then, he would later realize just how critical this power would become.

He walked down the street with crowds of people his age who had also been there. Yes, the others had parents, and he did not. And yes, the others had houses to go home to, and he did not. Yet none of that weighed him down in light of the unmistakable conviction he had that God was with him. Instead of worry, he felt peace. Instead of abandonment, he felt companionship. And most of all, instead of bitter hatred, he felt the first inklings of love, strange as it seemed, for his irresponsible parents.

That night he knelt down by his bed and talked to a Person he could not see. It was easy to thank God for loving him. That was no problem. It was easy to pray about the relief he felt that he was no longer some throwaway child. But praying for his parents was not easy. Sure, telling God how terrible they were—that would have been easy. Telling God how much better his life would be if he would have had decent parents—that would have been easy, too. But inside he knew they didn't have what he had. His father and mother were so far from the relationship with God he now had that, in spite of his deplorable childhood, he pushed himself to pray for them.

He prayed for God to change them, especially his father. Charles saw tremendous poverty in their lives, both physical and spiritual. It was as though some terrible curse had enveloped his parents, preventing them from knowing Christ. Charles made it a routine, every night, to pray for his parents—for them to see their need for God and for his father to stop his violent and abusive ways.

And the prayers made a difference.

Daudi became more responsible. He didn't fight as much. Didn't drink as much. But even though he hadn't hit Rhoda in over a month, she still walked in fear around him, the way women do when there is a history of violence in their marriages.

The government resettled Daudi, Rhoda and their children (except Charles) from Nakuru to the Machakos district. Along with other poor people in the cities, they were given bush land in a desolate area called Kathonzweni, which lies in the present-day Makueni district. Kathonzweni proved to be a glorified detention camp where impoverished people were given food to eat and a place to sleep. Later they were resettled to Ndalani, located 100 kilometres from Nairobi.

Charles, meanwhile, remained in Kathithyamaa. He continued with school and by 1967 finished standard (grade) eight. With no one to pay for high school fees, which were substantially more expensive than previous fees, Charles faced the possibility of not being able to continue the next year. And for a bright student like Charles, it seemed unfair. From standard one to four, he was first in his class. From standard five to eight, he was always in the top five. He had an unquenchable desire to go to university. He could do it. He knew he could. He had what it took. All he needed was money. He did what he could to ignore the burden of poverty on his shoulders as he wondered if his optimism could support his dreams.

He asked all his relatives for money to help with school fees. Being a beggar was nothing new for him, yet somehow it was worse having to go to people he knew. His relatives refused, giving him neither encouragement nor financial assistance. He was a brilliant child in search of a chance.

God, he prayed, *as I have been reading and learning in school, You see that I've never had a problem understanding things. Please God, don't let me become a slave to the people with whom I've been together in school. God, don't make me a beggar. God, use me and make me very prosperous. If You do that, I will do great work for You. God, help me, and I will do everything You ask, and I will be used by You. The first thing I will do is build a church.*

He had come to know that prayer made a difference. It wasn't just communication with God; it actually accomplished things. He had prayed for his father, whose behaviour was improving, though how long that would last was anybody's guess. Certainly prayer had made a difference, and Charles believed God would answer now as well.

In his short time as a follower of Christ, Charles was active in church. He became part of a local congregation, attended Bible studies, joined a Bible correspondence school where he earned a diploma, and pursued friendships with anyone he could. He was following God. Certainly God would see that and provide. Certainly God would answer the prayer for money from someone who was serving Him.

But the money never came.

The prayers, the service, the pursuit of Christ—none of it got Charles the money he needed to go on. He cried for two weeks. In the evening, when no one was around, maybe not even God (that's how it felt), he stayed on his bed awake, wondering how God, who at times could be so terribly generous, could at this point be so terribly stingy.

There was nothing more to do. There was no one else who could help. There was no other source of income. So Charles left his pursuit of schooling and went to find work.

He immediately went to neighbouring farms, where he dug holes. From early in the morning to late in the evening, he worked under the hot sun to get enough money to support himself. After three months he had money left over to buy shoes, trousers and a shirt for himself. He bought sugar and some food for his mother, saved the rest of his money and went to Ndalani to visit his parents.

It had been two years since he had last seen his family. He wondered what they looked like. He wondered what his brothers sounded like now that they were grown up. Would they be happy to see him? Had Father poisoned them with lies about him? He walked miles down the dusty, hot road from the highway to his parents' home. His eyes scanned the distance for any sign of them. There was bush everywhere. The area was dangerous, not from people but from animals. Poisonous snakes hid in the bushes and around rocks. Hippos, fat and lazy as they seemed, posed an imminent threat to anyone who had the misfortune of stumbling into their paths. And leopards, vicious creatures that could easily run down any prey, roamed the area looking for unsuspecting people to devour.

The sun began to set. The red glow barely gave off enough light for him to see his mother in the distance. He immediately felt different. In spite of all that had happened, in spite of all the abandonment, he felt the bond between mother and child that is not easily broken. She didn't appear to be injured. That was his first thought. His second thought was how tattered her clothes were. Her face was tired, showing the effects of physical and emotional hardship. She looked up from her work and saw her son approaching down the path to their home.

She closed her eyes, hoping that what she was seeing was not the effect of a long day on her imagination. Charles smiled. She cried. Her boy looked so sharp. Shoes, trousers and a shirt. All items she had not provided for him. He had managed to do it on his own. He had managed to take care of himself, to raise himself. All without her help.

And in that moment, she felt like a failure.

He hugged her, and she felt both the shame of not having done more for him and the joy in seeing him after such a long time. She didn't mind the tears. With a man like Daudi around, tears like this didn't come very often. If ever. Whether they were because of the guilt or because of the happiness, she did not know. Charles assumed it was the latter, which was just as well, because after the bitter disappointment with school and a long trip to see his mother, he needed to know she was as happy to see him as he was to see her.

Seeing his brothers again was as charging as it had always been. Seeing his father again was not. They exchanged greetings as they made eye contact. No hug. No smile. No happy tone in either of their voices. Instead of seeing an abusive father, Charles saw a man in desperate need of help. While Daudi still carried with him the threat of turning violent at any moment, Charles saw within him utter hopelessness and emptiness. He was a shell of a man without anything inside. Daudi was already dead.

He just didn't know it.

Charles put up a small brick house with a thatched roof for himself next to his parents. He spent what money he had left on food for the family. But when the money ran out, he knew it was time for him to move on. No sense in being a burden. But this time he would leave with a proper goodbye, or as proper a goodbye as he could get from his father, and not simply wake up one morning to abandonment.

He left his parents, without any idea of where he would go. He thought about going back to work digging on the farms. But how long could he do that? And what would it bring him in the long term? He would be able to survive, but if he wanted to truly help his family—and he did—he would have to do more.

He would have to search for work in Nairobi.

He made it to the river and paid the boat operator his half a shilling for the ride over to the other side. It was all the money he had left. Behind him was his family and in front of him was his future. What it would be like, he had no idea.

He stepped off the boat and started the three-day walk to Nairobi.

"God, take care of me," he prayed. "I don't know anybody in the city."

CHAPTER 8

The walk to Nairobi seemed longer than it really was, because he was making the journey alone. He spent the first night with his grandmother in Kathithyamaa and the second night on the side of the road beside a building. But when he got up on the third day and began the final stretch to Nairobi, the challenge of finding a job and a place to live became all the more apparent. This was no longer a trip to the capital of Kenya. It was a fight for survival. He continued to pray, continued to have courage and, as best he could, refused to entertain thoughts that he would end up a beggar in this large city that was not welcoming to newcomers.

The closer he got to the city, the more people he saw. They were everywhere. Crowding the streets. Crowding the market areas. It was packed. People shouted back and forth trying to sell things, enticing those walking by to stop and buy something. All along the sides of the street, people ran their simple businesses. Some were on blankets with their goods spread out in front of them. Some had small stands made of metal siding. They sold corn, drinks, shoes and fruit. There was everything here for the traveller.

At least for those who had money.

He arrived in the middle of the day and stopped at the side of the street near what is known today as Methodist Avenue. He looked in every direction, seeing nothing that looked familiar or welcoming. Along the way he imagined the kind of work he would have, where he would live, the friends he would have. But now that he was in the city, the dreaming stopped. It was time to find out what the future held for him.

He walked down the road and saw a large home protected by a fence and a gate. The larger the better, Charles thought. If they were as rich as they looked, they would have servants, and perhaps they were looking for additional help.

He stood at the gate, looking through at the activities inside. There was a large yard surrounding the beautiful home. In the distance he saw a small house that he assumed was the servants' quarters. Off to the other side he saw people preparing food and another person folding laundry. He knocked on the gate and wondered how many houses he would have to visit before he found work.

A servant came to the door. He looked older than Charles and studied him for a moment, as if doing so could unveil the motive behind why this exhausted young man was standing at the gate.

"Hello," the servant said as more of a question than a greeting.

"Hello," Charles replied. "Could I see the owner?"

"Do you know them?"

"No," Charles said. "I want to ask for work. Please get the owner."

The man waited a moment and turned without saying a word. Charles watched him disappear into the house and waited for any sign of the owner. It took so long for anyone to come that he wondered if the man had purposefully forgotten and left him standing there.

Then he saw her. A young Indian woman with curly black hair, wearing a skirt and a navy blue blouse, came out of the house giving instructions to one of the servants before coming to the gate. He tried to make eye contact with her while she was still a ways off, and what he saw in her gave him hope. While appearance doesn't often reveal the character of a person, Charles had the immediate impression this woman was both confident and compassionate. It was in the way she walked. The way she carried herself. There was something about her that gave Charles a glimmer of hope, the kind that comes when a person thinks things may just work out the way they wanted them to.

She came to the gate and smiled. Charles felt relieved.

"Young man," she said. "What can I do for you?"

"I'm looking for a job," he said wondering if that gate would remain locked or if she would soon be opening it for him.

"What kind of job?"

"Any kind of job," Charles said in a confident voice that conveyed he was both willing and capable of doing any job she needed him to do.

"How old are you?"

"Eighteen."

All these questions were a good sign. If she didn't have any jobs available, she would have told him by now and he would be on his way. But she was still speaking with him which meant there was something available, and each answer he gave, even something so seemingly small as the tone in his voice, was forming an opinion in her mind of the character inside this person behind the gate. Although it was only a few seconds before she asked her next question, to Charles it felt infinitely longer. Would she invite him in, or was she just stalling because she had already made up her mind about not hiring him? He looked into her eyes.

"Would you be able to cut grass?" she asked.

A rush of energy ran through Charles' veins. She was interested. He was so close to a job now, he felt he was already working there.

"Yes," he said. "I can cut grass. I have often used a sickle for such work."

"Can you weed my garden?"

"Absolutely."

"Trim the hedges."

"Yes."

She nodded slightly as if to give approval both for the courage this man had in asking for a job and for his willing demeanour.

"Tell me, do you know how to wash clothes?"

"Yes," Charles said. "I'm ready to do any job."

She smiled. It made Charles feel good. She opened the door.

"Welcome to my home," she said. "Please, come in."

Charles walked out from the city street, through the gate and on to her property. Not bad, he figured. One application. One job offer.

"You can stay in the servants' quarters," she said. "I will arrange for you to have a bed."

"Thank you," Charles said. *A bed? Is that what she said? Is she giving me my own bed?*

"And you will have your meals here as well. Those will be prepared for you."

"Thank you," he said, feeling that he was getting far more than he could have imagined. *Food? She's going to provide meals for me, too?*

"And you will be paid one American dollar per month. Is that all right with you?"

She stopped to look at him. Charles had a hard time believing it. He said nothing at first. How could he?

"That's fine," he whispered.

"I am Mrs. D'Souza," she said. "My husband and I live here with our two children, Eric and Colin."

"My name is Charles Mulli."

"Welcome, Charles. The head servant will tell you what to do."

She left him standing in the yard. He looked around. Not ten minutes earlier he had absolutely nothing. And now he had everything. A bed. Food. A job. What more could he ask for?

God had come through.

His first meal was rice. He ate it together with the other servants and by the end of lunch he had made friends with them. He was assigned numerous tasks. He had to cut three acres of grass with a sickle, trim the hedge, wash clothes, hang them out to dry and wash dishes.

That night he met Cirion D'Souza, an executive in a company that had sisal and coffee plantations. He and his wife were Christians and often spent time talking and joking around with him, making him feel he wasn't just the hired help but a person worth getting to know. They gave him permission to go home on occasion and to go to church as well.

It was evening when Mrs. D'Souza came out to talk to Charles. He had been there five months and had already proven himself to be the best servant. He was reliable in everything he did.

He heard her coming as he pulled down the last of the laundry from the line. He turned and smiled. She sat down on a bench and motioned for him to join her. It was a quiet evening. Their soft voices were all that separated them from silence.

"What do you want to do in life, Charles?" she asked.

It caught him off guard. Not that he didn't know how to answer. He knew what he wanted. It was just that it was new for him to have someone ask him about his future plans.

"I want to study," he said.

"Study."

"Yes."

"I admire that. It's important to have dreams."

"Sometimes I think that's all they will be."

"You are intelligent, Charles."

"Is intelligence enough?"

"You have a bright future."

"How can you know that?"

"Because I know you."

"But I have no opportunity."

"Do you think opportunity is found only in studying?"

Charles thought about his answer. The perfect calm felt like a sea of glass. "I have to study. I love to study. How else will I get a job?"

"So your plan is to study so that you can find better work?"

"Yes, Mrs. D'Souza."

"What if there was a way to get a better job without studying?"

"How is that possible?"

"Nothing is impossible to those who believe."

"But all the companies are looking for people who have finished university."

"University is a long and difficult road. You would have to finish primary school first and then complete secondary school. Then, if you were among the highest, you could go on to university. Not an easy task."

"I would make it," Charles said.

"This would take you eight, maybe ten, years to complete."

"It is a long road…"

"But it's not the only road."

Charles turned his head to look at her. She was hinting at something; he felt it, but he wasn't sure what it was. "How else would I find a position?"

"You're much too smart to be working here forever, Charles. This is no place for you."

"Without university, I won't be able to move on."

She stood up, put her hand on his shoulder and looked deep into his eyes. "We'll have to see about that."

A month later, Mr. D'Souza called him to the backyard and asked him to join him at the table. Charles sat down.

"I have good news for you," he said.

Charles smiled, expecting, perhaps, that D'Souza was talking about a raise.

"You have a new job," he said. That was good news. "In Makuyu."

"Makuyu?"

"I got you a job as a field clerk. You will be responsible for going to the field and collecting the names of the people who have come to work. You will need to mark down the attendance, prepare payments and make sure everything has been entered into the books. How does that sound?"

Charles couldn't reply. A job as a field clerk? Without even applying for the job? He looked at Mr. D'Souza and felt the thrill of a new challenge and the wonder of receiving something that was totally unexpected.

"Thank you," he said.

In September 1968, Charles started his job for Kakuzi Fibreland Ltd. He was young and talented, which was noticed by all the employees, who felt threatened that this newcomer would take over their jobs. He worked harder and longer hours than the other workers. It didn't take him long to become a supervisor, and soon after he was promoted to assistant manager. He climbed the ladder faster than anyone. And with each step came an increase in pay. For the first time he could consider buying a vehicle.

Day and night he lived and breathed his job, making every effort to concentrate on getting ahead. He pushed longer and longer hours and made even wiser use of his time. He took on more challenges and added to his own job description, to prove to himself and his bosses that he was easily the best man for the job. All his work made it difficult for him to think about anything else in life.

A young woman he was about to meet would change all that.

CHAPTER 9

Charles walked along a path between fields, holding his book containing the names of the workers. He checked off those who were in the fields. He'd only been there six months, but already he had gotten to know them. All 1,200. He knew their names and would often stop to talk with people to inquire about their lives, their families and their interests. But on this occasion, when he came to a young woman working in the field picking pineapples, he realized he had an instant interest in her beyond what he had ever encountered before.

She was slender. And out of all the workers on the farm, she was different. The field was packed with people, but to Charles she was the only one there. He watched, magnetized to her presence, feeling the unstoppable attraction that comes when a man is captivated by a woman. She didn't notice him. Not at first. He stood there, staring at her, unable to break his concentration. Even under the relentless sun, Charles felt frozen, focusing on her as he watched her work.

She looked up from her work and saw him looking at her. She was young. Gorgeous eyes and a compelling face. He walked towards her, feeling the pounding in his chest. It was his job to know her. This was all part of his work. He had never seen her before, and he had to find out her name in order to ensure that she got properly paid. He was, after all, being paid to keep track of who was in the field. It was his duty to speak with her.

"Hello," he said, quieter than he would have liked. It didn't sound very commanding, didn't sound like he was in charge. But he couldn't help it. She hadn't said a word to him, hadn't even reacted to him, and still she had conveyed something that made him wonder if this was an encounter he would never forget.

"Hello," she replied.

Her voice was soft and comforting. There was a quiet confidence about her that made Charles wish he didn't have to ask work-related questions.

"I haven't seen you here before," Charles said, convincing her he was glad she had come.

"It's my first day," she said. "I'm working here for my mother. She's sick today."

Charles wanted to say he was sorry to hear that. But on this day, and with this woman, having her mother sick was the best thing that could have happened to him.

She wore a grey headscarf and a long dress. It made him wonder what a woman like this was doing working in the field.

"I'm sorry to hear that," he finally managed to get out. "How old are you?"

"Fifteen."

Something inside Charles was connecting with this young woman. And he hoped it wouldn't be the last time he would see her.

"My name is Charles Mulli."

She smiled again. "I'm Esther."

The next day he hurried through the field, rushing as he checked off the names, completing his list in the shortest amount of time yet. People tried to stop him to get his attention, but he refused to slow down. He gave shorter greetings and faster smiles to the people and did everything he could to avoid conversation. He had someone else to speak with— and as he got to that same field, his eyes scanned the workers, looking for someone in particular.

There she was. Esther. Working in the field. The sun shone down on her as though it were a spotlight meant just for her. He felt the relief a man feels when he knows he has another chance to make further ground with the woman he's interested in. As he walked closer, he barely heard the greetings of workers right beside him. His eyes, determined and purposeful, stayed locked on her. He felt the power of attraction with every step he took. She sensed his presence. And in that moment when she turned from her work to look up at him, he felt a sudden jolt of fear, wondering if they truly had something between them or if yesterday was just a fluke.

Her smile instilled confidence in Charles as he came to her. Without even saying a word she had managed to find the path into his heart in a way only a woman can.

She told him her parents were divorced because of a dowry problem and the resulting financial problems meant she wasn't able to go to school. Charles admired her for helping with the family finances and felt compassion towards her because she, like him, was not able to further her education.

She told him she stayed with her mother not far from where Charles lived. Their home was in a poor area. Low class. Just above slum conditions.

Not long afterward, the company hired Esther on as a labourer, enabling them to see each other more often.

Charles and Esther often met riding their bicycles. They talked, especially Esther, who proved to have a coveted combination of sincerity and laughter. When he went to the market, Esther saw how everyone knew him. He was the young boss that people loved. People constantly stopped him to speak with him and to hear his advice on their personal problems. A crowd of young ladies, thirty of them, danced in a circle around him singing, "*Mulli, Mulli, Mulli*," shouting out, "*Kori!*," meaning "a small lamb." From her house, Esther saw all the dancing and realized that from all the women who adored Charles, he had chosen her.

Charles often took the bus into downtown Nairobi on business. He spent the mornings taking care of work-related concerns, and even though he had a mountain of work piling up, he made time to speak with street boys. They were Nairobi's growing population of throwaway children. Their parents had either died or were hooked on drugs or were too poor to take care of them. Many of the children took to the streets for survival, to eek out whatever source of revenue they could. Some of them joined gangs where they stole to buy food. Sometimes girls worked as prostitutes to fund their miserable existence. In the evenings they sometimes slept on sidewalks or under the overhangs of supermarkets, if the security guards let them.

On one occasion, Charles saw a small group of street boys walking together. Torn, ragged clothing. Ripped shoes. Dirty faces. But their most distinguishing feature was the look of desperation in their eyes. Their eyes weren't bright, like Esther's. They were dull, with a faint glimmer at best. Their eyes told their life stories and what they thought their chances were of getting out of the lowest social position. In those small windows to their souls, Charles saw the same pain, frustration and lack of hope he often saw in his own eyes when, as a boy, he would look into the mirror.

He walked up to them, smiled, stretched out his hands palm up and gave what became his trademark greeting. "*Ooo-aye!*"

They looked at him and wondered what this well-dressed man, who wasn't that much older than they were, wanted with them.

"Hello," he said.

No response. Not a smile. Not a hello. All he got was a look from their lifeless eyes.

"Why are you in the street?" he asked.

The shortest one looked up at the one beside him as if to ask approval before volunteering an answer. He looked back at Charles. "Where else are we going to go?" he said.

"Do you have enough food to eat?" Charles asked.

One of them shook his head.

"A place to sleep?"

They didn't need to give him an answer.

As he talked with them he felt their pain, knowing they were in a place they didn't want to be and were powerless to change it. He went to a nearby store and bought them some bread. He gave it to them. They nearly ripped it out of his hands. Charles watched as they began to eat. Then he turned and left.

But he was not able to put the street children out of his mind.

It was when Esther left to work as a housemaid in Nairobi that Charles knew she was the one for him. Seeing her so often had given him the conviction that she was unlike anyone he had ever met. Now that she was away, it only served to convince him that he loved her.

He sat down in his chair and felt the loneliness that comes when a man senses the emptiness left by the woman in his life. He prayed about whether she was, in fact, the woman for him. How does a man ever really know for sure? But there was something deep inside, in that place where people know things for certain, that told him she was not only the woman he wanted but also the woman he needed. He got out his pen and paper and wrote her a letter, inviting her to come and visit him.

He had gone over his line, the big question, numerous times. He practiced it out loud over and over again so that when the time came it would come out just right. Back and forth he paced in his living room area, wondering what her reaction would be. A knock at the door. His heart pounded. He swallowed and took a deep breath to calm his nerves. He had it all worked out. All ready to go. But when he opened the door and looked into the eyes of who he believed would be his future wife, his mind suddenly went blank.

There was Esther. Standing with her infectious smile and glistening eyes. He wanted to say something, yet he hesitated. Being in the presence of a fascinating woman prevented him from giving an immediate greeting.

"Esther," he said. So far so good.

"Hello, Charles." There was something unique in the way she said his name.

"I'm glad you've come."

"Thank you for inviting me."

"Would you like to take a walk?"

Eight people came to Esther's home on December 22, 1970, to celebrate the wedding of Charles and Esther. She was seventeen. He was twenty-one. Daudi and Rhoda came, thanks to money for transportation from Charles. Esther's grandmother supervised the vows, and as Charles said "I do" he had the undeniable feeling that he was a present to Esther.

And that she was a present to him.

According to their Kamba tribe tradition, the wife had to live with her in-laws, so Esther went to live with Daudi and Rhoda. Charles took a position with Strawbag and was transferred from Makuyu to Eldoret. The increase in pay allowed Charles to buy his first car—a second-hand Ford Cortina. He was the first person in his family and in Ndalani to own a vehicle. He came to visit his wife and family every month and brought with him a jukebox to play his music. He often sat with his new wife, talking about her life and his job while listening to Jimmy Reeves sing one of Charles' favourite songs: "This world is not my home. I'm just a-passing through."

CHAPTER 10

By the time their first child, Jane, was born, Esther's life at Daudi and Rhoda's home had begun to unravel.

Tradition aside, there was no longer any point for her to be there. Daudi had turned back to his old ways. Booze. Anger. Violence. What Charles had assumed was behind them came crashing back into their lives.

"Where is the rest of the money?" Daudi screamed. He was drunk. Again. And he was yelling. Again.

Rhoda tried to calm him down. But her pleas never seemed to matter, especially not when he was in this condition.

"Charles sends money every month, Daudi," she said, hoping to calm him down. "Next month there will be more money."

"Next month! Next month!" That was a long time to go without booze (or food) money. He clenched his teeth together. But that didn't bother Rhoda. Clenched teeth were never a problem. Clenched fists, however, were a different matter entirely.

Esther backed away from Daudi and picked up baby Jane from the bed. The other sons were home. They would step in if Daudi became violent. Whether they would succeed in defeating their enraged father was anybody's guess.

"Next month he will bring more money," Rhoda said again.

"He better! He never brings enough! Never!"

Charles was giving 60 percent of his salary to his parents, leaving him hardly anything to get ahead with after all his expenses in the city.

And Daudi? He gave nothing. Not a penny. He didn't find work (didn't look for it either), and while his son worked eighteen-hour days to make ends meet for two households, Daudi spent Charles' money on alcohol as he watched his wife, sons, daughter-in-law and new granddaughter suffer in poverty.

"I will talk to him," Rhoda said, following Esther. She closed the door behind them and breathed a quiet sigh of relief that he had not turned violent.

For now.

Esther was the first to begin crying. She pinched her eyelids together, trying to hold back the emotion, hoping to cling to those last remaining optimistic thoughts she had about what married life would be like. But those dreams were vanishing, and she felt the pain new wives feel when they realize the life they had wished for is no longer within reach.

Rhoda put one arm around Esther and the other on Jane, who slept in peace, unaware of the turmoil in which she was growing up. Rhoda didn't cry. She'd been here before. She'd been here while Charles was a boy. She'd been here with the other sons. She'd been here countless times by herself. Now, Esther and Jane were joining in on the family tradition of misery and pain. She said nothing to Esther under the canopy of stars. What was there to say? She wanted to say things would get better.

But Rhoda was not one to lie.

The three of them slept outside under a tree on a blanket. It was cold. It was uncomfortable.

But it was a far cry better than living with Daudi.

"I can't stay here," Esther said to Charles during one of his monthly visits. Her voice was filled with the panic that consumes people who are seeking a way out of a situation they no longer control. "Your father..." she started.

"What?" Charles said, feeling the exhaustion of a long drive from his new position located in the city of Eldoret near the Uganda border.

"Your father steals the money you bring here."

They were down by the river. It was quiet. Evening was approaching. He had no reason to doubt his wife. And he had no reason to hold his father in high regard.

"He spends the money on alcohol and cigars," she said. Every word she said took effort. It was as though she was pleading with Charles to finally do something. "There's nothing left for us. This is worse than poverty."

The first thing that bothered Charles about this situation was the conditions his wife and child were living in. They didn't deserve this. There was no reason for it. His own wife and child living the same way he grew up. No food. A horrible father figure. It was history repeating itself. The second thing that bothered him was all the hard-earned money that was wasted. For what? *For what?* For nothing. The money he earned made it *worse* for his family. Not only did they have nothing to begin with, but the money they did receive was being used by Daudi for alcohol, which brought out his terrible side, making things that much more unbearable.

And it was now enough.

"We have to talk," Charles said.

They sat alone at a table out in the field. Out of shouting distance from the rest of the family. Daudi was sober, or as sober as a drunk gets when he has a steady supply of money and booze.

"How's work?" Daudi asked. But Charles knew what he really meant. The comment should have been an indication of a father's genuine interest in his son's welfare. But what Daudi was after was knowing whether his alcohol money would be coming in next month.

"Work is fine. How is the work situation with you?"

That cut right into Daudi. His face flushed. He was ready to turn the table over, reach out to grab his son and beat him unconscious. And he would have, but he controlled himself. No point in destroying his only source of income.

"You know how it is," Daudi said, putting on a fake smile. "Difficult times." He added a short laugh. But the void in his eyes told Charles what was truly going on, or not going on, in his father's life. They were so empty. Shells, really. As lifeless as the eyes on a doll.

"You've been receiving the money I've sent you?"

"Yes. It's been helpful."

"Helpful."

"Yes. Very helpful."

"How?"

"How?"

"Yes, Father. How has my money been helpful?"

Daudi smiled again to reveal his toothless grin, but still it did little to lighten the mood. "Your money helps us."

"I want to know how it helps you." Charles' voice became more intense. More commanding. He was like a police officer in an interrogation who has turned from asking questions to demanding answers. "Tell me, Father. How exactly does my money help the family?"

Daudi was quiet. This was the first time anyone in the family had dared challenge him on anything. And Daudi felt threatened, the way people do when they know they've been lying and are about to be exposed.

"We buy things."

"Like what?"

"Things for the family."

"Clothing?"

"Yes, clothing."

"Food?"

"Yes, food."

"School fees?"

"Yes. All of those things."

Charles leaned forward. He looked right into his father's deathly cold eyes. He studied them a moment, as if doing so could enable him to speak directly into Daudi's spirit.

"You are lying."

Daudi froze. He didn't know what to do. Start fighting, or try to talk his way out? Did this mean the money would not be coming?

"I'm not lying," Daudi said, in a tone devoid of any conviction.

"What do you spend the money on?"

"I told you."

"No. You told me nothing but what you thought I wanted to hear!" Charles took a deep breath to help calm himself down. "Now tell me exactly—how are you spending the money for which I work long hours? Day and night and night and day I slave away at my job, for what?" He slammed his fist down on the table. It scared Daudi. He felt threatened by one of his own.

But even with the evidence staring him in the face, Daudi was unable to speak the truth. It was booze. He knew it. Charles knew it. Everybody knew it. But there was something inside Daudi that would not let it out. As obvious as it was, the truth would remain hidden. He wouldn't let it out, even if the only purpose it served was to let himself continue believing his own lie.

"And when you get your alcohol, what do you do when you're drunk?"

Silence. Every word Charles said felt like a whip against Daudi's back.

"You get drunk, and then you start hitting Mother again. I hear the stories. I know what's happening here. And I have now had it with you."

Daudi suddenly found a resolve within him that had remained hidden up until now. He gathered up what little self-esteem he had left and looked his son in the eye. "You're not talking this way to me on my own property. You're going to continue bringing me my money."

"Quiet."

And in that instant Daudi lost all his power over Charles. Daudi looked away, feeling more like a delinquent son than a self-centred father.

"This has gone on far too long. You treat Mother worse than an animal would treat its prey. Here is what is going to happen. Are you listening to me?" Daudi said nothing. He looked so pathetic, so defeated, sitting in that chair. "I'm taking Esther and Jane back with me to Eldoret." That ripped Daudi in half. It was his right—his right—to have Esther at his home, and having Charles take her away meant Daudi could disown him. But that tradition had little power considering who was taking care of whom. "And this is the last time that I am warning you about Mother."

Daudi had heard this before, too. Empty threats followed by his own empty promises that he would change, which he never did. At least not for long. And so Daudi tuned Charles out.

Until he heard how Charles was going to back up his instruction for him to stop destroying Rhoda.

"You know the clan rules, don't you?"

Paralysis hit Daudi. Clan rules. Clan rules. It echoed in his drunken mind. He knew the clan rules. Everyone knew the clan rules. His fingers began to tremble as his body realized what could happen to him if he had to face the clan. He swallowed and wished he could disappear from his son's presence.

"If I hear you are beating Mother again, I will write to the clan and have them deal with you."

It was as though someone had screamed in Daudi's ear to make him shudder.

"They will haul you into an assembly and hear the testimony of witnesses—every single one of whom will be happy to tell of all the horrors you have committed against her."

Daudi cringed. He turned away from Charles, but it did little to cushion the impact of the words he was about to hear.

"And when the clan finds you guilty, and they will, they will stretch you out on the ground and tie you face down with cords. Then the young, strong men in the village will take turns whipping you with carefully trimmed heavy branches. Your skin will split open. Blood will fly out in all directions. You'll scream as bad as mother has all these years, but no one will care. No one will come to your aid. In fact, help will be only a few arm lengths away, but instead of the community reaching out to help you, they will be applauding as they watch you suffer. They will look at you in your agony and be happy about it. Then, once the branches have ripped away your skin, they will smash them against your bare spine and you will feel pain that very few people on earth ever experience. Your body will shake uncontrollably. You'll throw up from all the torture. Screaming. Yelling. Begging for it stop. But it won't. It will go on. And when the branches finally cut through your spine, you will die. And the whole village will look at your disgusting, lifeless body and feel the justice that comes with knowing a wife-beater like you finally got what he deserved."

Daudi trembled the way Charles used to when he waited on his bed late at night for him to come home and beat them. They waited in silence. There was nothing left to say.

Charles stood up from the table and left. Minutes passed as Daudi sat there, realizing the potential consequences of his fragile inability to keep any promise. Charles drove off in his car. Daudi didn't look up. He couldn't. All he could do was feel the weight of his conscience and know that his life was now hanging by his volition to stay away from alcohol.

And from Rhoda.

Esther and Jane came by train to Eldoret. The day-long trip was quiet. Jane slept most of the way. With every kilometre, Esther felt the release of being physically removed from a disastrous situation. The air felt cleaner. She found it easier to breathe. A real life. A real marriage with the man she loved and admired was coming closer with every turn of the train's wheels.

When the train slowed down on its approach into Eldoret, Esther leaned closer to the window, clutching young Jane in her arms, searching for Charles. They came to a stop. People had gathered along the track, looking for their families and friends. She saw him standing among the crowd. The brightness in his eyes convinced her that she was now starting over. The anxiety of living in constant fear was behind her.

And what lay before her was an adventure she could never have dreamed.

CHAPTER 11

Charles resigned from his position at Strawbag. The company received a construction contract in Yemen and wanted Charles to go. But his desire to make a home in Kenya with his young family and a pressing interest to start his own business kept him in Eldoret.

He thought about how he had been so blessed by God. His family. His career. His prosperity. He had come so far. From an orphan beggar to a company executive. How does that happen, apart from God's working? But as much as he had accomplished, somehow Charles knew there was even more on the horizon for him. He took the severance package, walked out the door and began planning his first business.

"You want to do what?" Esther asked.

"A matatu business," Charles said.

"You left your job?" Esther questioned as she tried to disguise the touch of fear in her voice, knowing their family was now without a secure job.

"Yes."

"To start a business?"

"That's right. I'm going to convert our van into a matatu."

Matatus come in all sizes, but normally they are passenger vans run by private individuals who drive people on various routes throughout a city, like a cross between a taxi and a transit bus. Matatus could comfortably carry fourteen people, but it wasn't unusual to see twenty or more crammed inside. Sometimes passengers hung out the sides or onto the back bumper.

In April 1973, Charles converted his pickup truck to a matatu by putting a canvas over the top and building benches in the box portion to act as seats. He then rented a house beside a camp of homes belonging to Strawbag employees and pioneered a route from there to Eldoret. He got up early the first morning and drove his new matatu to the first stop. A small group of workers got on, paid the fare and sat down. He put the car in gear, let out the clutch and started down the road.

Charles Mulli was in business.

Within days his matatu was full. People crammed in line waiting for a chance to get a ride with Charles. He played Christian music, a rarity at the time, which gave his matatu experience a unique feature. He got to know his customers by name and made it a habit to address each of them as they came on board. To make his bus more distinguishable, Charles painted his new company logo on the side: Mullyways.

While his last name ended in an *i*, Charles spelled the corporate name with a *y* to distinguish it from personal finances.

Now, when he got on his matatu, he felt the pride of having his name associated with the business. His dream was coming true. He was starting out small. His entire company consisted of just one small van.

But little did he know where it would take him

With the very first signs of profit, Charles used what little money he could spare to help street children in Eldoret. While both the businesses and his family could have benefited from the extra money, he chose to keep a watchful eye out for anyone who could use his help.

"Hello," he said to three boys standing around a garbage can. It had been filled with rags and set on fire for them to stay warm. It was early. They were cold. They were dirty.

They were hungry.

They made no response. Why should they? What was in it for them? If this crazy man got out of his van, perhaps they would beat him up, take his watch and rummage through his clothes to find money.

Mulli stopped his van. There weren't many people out. Farther away, store owners began opening their shops for the day. But where the boys were, at the end of the street away from everyone else, things looked different. They were by themselves, on their turf. If something went wrong, it might be too late for Charles to summon help.

"Are you hungry?" he asked.

Still no reply. The boys looked at each other. *Who is this man? What is his problem? Just get back in your matatu and go earn your money. What do you want with us?*

Charles got close enough to see the emptiness in their eyes. Shells of desperation that reflected what little light came from the flames. They squinted their eyes, as if able to see some faint glimmer of hope in Charles. That's when they noticed the bag he was holding. Somehow their suspicion of his presence made them unable, or unwilling, to see anything benevolent in that package.

"I have something for you boys," he said.

Their eyes focused on the bag. Perhaps he was a policeman tricking them into giving them their attention while other officers surrounded them. One of them turned around and scanned the area to make sure that wasn't the case. Or perhaps this man was just plain out of his mind, drunk after a long evening and wanted to share some of his booze with them. That would be all right. That would be the best. Alcohol. Marijuana. It was all a blessing for them. A chance to ignore the pain. A chance to escape. A chance to numb the ache of abandonment and despair.

But that was not going to be the case.

Not tonight.

Instead, Mulli reached into the bag and pulled out two loaves of bread.

"I brought these for you. You must be hungry. It's cold so early in the morning, isn't it? Where did you sleep last night?"

The look on their faces was their answer.

"Here," he said, offering them the bread.

The tallest boy stretched out his hand in a noncommittal sort of way so as to be able to draw it back in case there would be trouble. He touched the loaves of bread. It was more than they had eaten in three days. Two whole loaves.

Two whole loaves.

He took the first and gave it to the one next to him. Then he reached out and took the second. Charles smiled, and then he laughed.

"It's good bread. Fresh. I just bought it."

Why? Why is this man doing this? What is wrong with him? Is he a shop owner? Does he recognize us as the ones who stole from him? Is he trying to get a better look at us so he can point us out to the police? Why would he just give bread away like this?

"*Assante,*" they said, meaning "thank you."

"You're welcome," he said.

There was a long silence between them, each side wondering what the other thought of them. Sometimes those periods of quiet can feel awkward as people search for words to say. But for three street boys who were encountering the generosity of a stranger, it was a stillness in which to receive something from a person who wanted nothing in return.

"I will see you again," Charles said. "And I will bring more bread."

They nodded. They were not used to being shown kindness and were unsure of how to respond.

Charles got back into his matatu and started his fourteen-hour day.

Business boomed for Charles. Day and night, passengers overcrowded the vehicle, squishing against one another to make room for yet one more person who pleaded to be squeezed in. With the money he earned from the matatu business, he and Esther rented a shop at the end of the road in Nyaru to sell vegetables, sodas, food and clothes. Even though he was the only man from the Kamba tribe in Nyaru, he was accepted culturally.

Using instalment plans he purchased additional vehicles to supply the expanding demand on his routes. Like a huge catch of fish in a fisherman's net, Charles' matatus burst with people trying to get a ride. It was as if the passengers were metal and his vans magnets.

But just when he thought he had managed to get his business to a stable position, he had to use all of his money to pay for vehicle repairs. Everything he had saved up, gone. A wife, a child, the pressures of business, everything weighed on him like a heavy pack on an uphill climb. Yet he had an uncanny confidence that God would come through for him. Somehow, someway, He would do it. Even when the expenses piled up and appeared to outweigh the projected income, he had the strange ability to believe that in spite of what he was seeing, things were going to work out.

In 1976, he forced himself to drive his matatu for three days and nights straight. No sleep. No rest. The cheerful, smiling Charles Mulli had been replaced with a man hardly able to remember his own name. The passengers came aboard; he nodded, accepted their fares and drove off to Kisumu. He forced his eyes to stay open, but like a child way past his bedtime, Charles couldn't stay awake any longer. He finally pulled over to the side of the road and told his passengers he needed to sleep.

Half an hour was all he took.

He got back on the road at 3:00 a.m. and drove to Eldoret, arriving on December 24. He dropped off his passengers and, unable to distinguish between morning and evening, managed to manoeuvre his way through traffic back to his home. He got out of the van, his legs nearly giving way, and staggered to the house.

Esther came to the door. When she heard the van pull up she expected to see a husband full of energy, ready to celebrate. Instead, she saw a man who had gone past the definitions of tired, exhausted and finished. She put her arms around him and brought him into the house and up to their bedroom. The last thing Charles saw was the fast-approaching bed as he crashed down on it. He fell asleep before landing. He lay there, with his shoes on, in a deep sleep. Dead to the world. For thirteen straight hours.

When he woke up at 10:00 that evening, he took a shower and ate with Esther. He talked with her about her day, the children and his three-day adventure. Then he got up, went outside to his matatu and went back to work.

In April of 1976, he closed his shop in Nyaru and reopened in Eldoret. By December, he had enough money to buy an eight-acre property, where he built a house and planted the first banana, orange, mango and passion fruit trees in Eldoret.

By 1977, he owned four matatus. He bought three more plots in Eldoret to build houses for rent. Everything he did worked out. Every deal he made turned in his favour. While some do not succeed for fear of failure, Charles knew no such fear. Collapse wouldn't happen. Couldn't happen. He had prayed. He had confidence.

He had success.

The challenges in Charles' life extended beyond his marriage, his children and his businesses. On top of those, Charles was consumed with the fate of his father and mother.

And as a man trapped in his ways, Daudi began beating Rhoda again.

It was obvious each time Daudi would come to visit Charles. Sometimes he would bring Rhoda; sometimes he would leave her at home for fear the marks would be too obvious. Charles paid for Daudi to visit. When he came and gave that toothless grin, Charles knew it didn't stem from love. When Daudi told him how proud he was, Charles knew the words were insincere. When Daudi spoke of the hardships in Ndalani, how difficult it was to make money and how hard he was trying, all Charles could hear was the same old story.

Daudi wanted money.

Which, in and of itself, would not have been the end of the world had Daudi used the money to help the family and not drink it away. The trouble was that when he drank, he still got violent.

And when he got violent, he had one favourite target.

Charles had purchased cows, sheep, a table, chairs and other items for their house in Ndalani. When the family money (the booze money) ran out, Daudi sold off the animals, and with them their livelihood, to maintain his addiction.

"Stop it!" Rhoda had pleaded with him, knowing that her husband—if that's what he could be called—was directly causing their financial, social and relational ruin.

"Shut up!"

Selling the animals and possessions was a problem. Rhoda trying to intervene was a problem, too. And inside, Daudi knew he wasn't the man he was supposed to be. Deep down in the part that gives a man his identity, Daudi had only a hollow void. He was nothing. He was no one. And as bad as that reality felt during the day, it had an uncanny way of expressing itself late at night after he had been drinking.

Charles drove down to see Daudi again. He had the incredible urge to summon his Aombe clan of the Kamba tribe to cast a final judgment on Daudi's life. It's what he deserved.

It's what he had earned.

Charles went to see his mother first. He thought that after all the times he had seen his mother beaten he would have gotten used to it. But he hadn't. And seeing the cuts and bruises on his mother's mangled and disfigured face made it impossible to let this go any further.

"We're putting a stop to this," Charles said.

Rhoda said nothing. It was as though she feared her fragile voice might carry through the wind, reach Daudi's ears and set him off in a diabolical rage.

"This is enough," Charles said.

"I've had it with you," Charles said in a stern and forceful tone.

Daudi played the victim and pressed his lips together. "I have had so much trouble. Things have been very difficult around here."

"Quiet. You've had your say," Charles said, trying hard to remain composed, or as composed as a man can be when his father is worse than a criminal. "I only have one thing to say to you."

Daudi didn't look up. He couldn't find the courage.

"You had better listen very carefully to what I'm going to tell you." Charles leaned closer. He waited until his father managed to make eye contact. What a pathetic man. What a worthless, fearful human being. Charles stared into those cold eyes, seeing nothing but emptiness. "If it happens again I'll report you to the clan."

And that was it. That's all he said. No temper. No anger. Sometimes a man can believe change in a terrible situation is possible. But Charles was past that. Heaven knew Rhoda was long since past that as well. There was no inflection in Charles voice to give Daudi the idea that Charles hoped he would finally turn his life around. Instead, Daudi felt the terror of knowing the only thing standing between him and being a bloodied corpse was one evening of drinking and a few swings at Rhoda.

Daudi felt regretful, which is a far cry from feeling remorseful. He regretted his circumstances, not his actions—his personal danger, not the damage done to his wife. He was afraid of the potential punishment but felt no sorrow over his deeds.

He had shot arrows at neighbours who came to tell him to change. He had chased his sons away when they tried to reason with him. He drank away his son's money. He sold their livelihood for more booze. He beat his wife. The choice was simple. The bottle or the clan?

Three months later, Charles received news that Rhoda and Muthikwa were coming from Eldoret. He met them at the train station, hoping against reason that this was going to be a pleasant surprise—that they wanted to come to see him and congratulate him on his success.

But when he saw Rhoda, all of that changed.

Her face was as bad as it had been before. Muthikwa had her arm around her to hold her up. Rhoda's head was so swollen it looked like a balloon that would suddenly burst. The discoloration in her face glistened in the sun as though someone had smeared dark paint all over her.

Charles hugged her as best he could without causing her more pain. The tears in Rhoda's eyes stung the bruising and blistering around them.

They sat down in his home and recounted the events. There was nothing new to tell. How many variations of *he got drunk and beat me* were there? Yet it was therapeutic for Rhoda, at least to some degree, to talk about it. Charles listened as she described the beatings, knowing he was hearing the final evidence he needed to summon his resolve and make the decision that weighed on his shoulders.

He left the room and sat down at his desk. It was quiet, except for his mother's crying that could be heard throughout the house. He pulled out a pen. It felt like a weapon in his hand, and perhaps it was. He got out a piece of paper. His own father. How could Charles do this? His very own father.

No. No, absolutely not. He was not a father. And he was certainly not a husband. He could be called a lot of things, but not father or husband.

But he was flesh and blood. *His* flesh and blood. This was family.

Did that somehow excuse it? Did that make it right? Was being family some sort of trump card or immunity against the consequences of what he was doing and would continue to do?

The burden of justice lay with Charles. And he was equal to the task.

He took in a deep breath, adjusted himself on the chair and began writing a letter to the chief of the clan asking for a full trial, knowing that it would cost his father his life.

CHAPTER 12

Daudi stood by himself in the shade. It was cool outside. He didn't need to be standing under a tree. But he knew what was coming. Today was going to be the longest day of his life, even though he wouldn't live to see the end of it. Normally, he would be recovering from a hangover this early in the morning. Normally, his hands wouldn't be trembling uncontrollably, his teeth wouldn't be chattering, sweat wouldn't be dripping off his face. Terror wouldn't be controlling his every thought.

Strange the effect an upcoming meeting with the clan leadership can have.

In an unexpected reaction, he suddenly felt his stomach heave as chunks of vomit flew out of his mouth. He got down on his knees and spit out the remaining pieces. A rush of heat raced through his forehead. He pulled a nearby pan of water closer to himself. He scooped some out and splashed it over his face to cool himself down. His breathing, his mind, his conscience all became heavier, as though he was carrying twice the weight he had been only moments earlier. He looked down at the pan and saw his reflection.

This is what death looked like.

"It is time," a voice said behind him.

Already? How could it be time? I just got up.

But he hadn't just gotten up. Hadn't even gone to sleep. Those on death row never could.

At least not the night before.

"All right," he said. He stood up, his legs feeling weak, as though they might fail him at any moment. "I'm coming."

He turned around and saw them standing there. Six of them. Strong. Young. Their eyes told Daudi they would be easy to deal with if he co-operated but merciless if he was trouble.

He had thought about running. He had thought about leaving. In the middle of the night. He could take off. Go somewhere. Anywhere. But how far could he get? No money. No food. He could have at most a six-hour start. That would be nothing if a manhunt came after him, tracking him down for trying to escape justice. If he was caught, and surely he would be, his chances of survival would be zero. Perhaps the clan would have mercy on him. Perhaps they would let him change his ways.

But as he went with the strong men he knew what awaited him. He knew what happened at these clan meetings. They all knew. And he knew why he was going. It was because of that son of his. That horrible, rotten Charles. Why couldn't he just give the money like he always did? Why did he have to write that letter? What business was it of his? How dare he meddle in his parents' lives like this?

It was all Charles' fault.

Charles waited with all the others under a large tree. The community, his brothers, his uncles and aunts and the clan leadership all stood waiting for Daudi to be brought in. For the leadership, this was about justice. For the community, it was a party. For the uncles, aunts and brothers, it was about Rhoda getting the freedom she deserved from the abuse she suffered.

For Charles, it was about holding a man responsible for the evil he had committed.

The young, strong men brought Daudi to the assembly. The crowd grew quiet as they became aware of the burden of life that was now among them.

It was a bright day. There should be children playing. People should be working in the fields. But there was none of that. Only silence as a dead man walked into their presence.

Charles was the only one who had the courage to look at Daudi. And the moment their eyes met, Charles felt Daudi's anger. Daudi glared at him. He clenched his teeth at him as if to say *if I could get away from the men I would tear you to pieces for how you have betrayed me. Look what you've done!*

A bull was tied up behind the tree. Like Daudi, it was ready to be killed. Once the young men had split Daudi's back open and killed him, it would be time to slaughter the bull. It would be time to put the past behind. It would be time for celebration.

"Charles Mulli," the chief said. He was a short man, but in spite of his limited height, he easily commanded the respect of everyone he ruled over. Charles stepped forward near his father, who was surrounded by the strong young men. And that comforted Charles. If Daudi turned crazy (again), it may not take him long to choke the life out of Charles.

"You are this man's son. Can you explain the problem?"

Side by side. Father and son. Accused and accuser. Death row and free man.

"This is my father. Ever since I can remember, he has beaten my mother." Charles paused. He was really doing this. He was really carrying through with his promise. Only months earlier he had talked, not far from here, with his father and told him this day was coming. And now it was here. "We have warned him for years. Telling him, pleading with him, commanding him to change."

Charles wanted to look to his left for effect, to see if his father had the pride, the arrogance, to stare at him now that the facts were being spelled out in front of him. Each statement felt like another brick being loaded onto his sinking ship.

"He has sold all the possessions, on numerous occasions, to drink. And when he drinks, he gets violent."

"With all of you?"

"Yes." Not that it mattered. Charles wasn't here to complain, or testify, about the beatings he and his brothers received. They were bad. Certainly. But he wanted it to be clear that this judgment, this trial, would be decided on the basis of what Daudi had done to their mother.

"There are three conditions," the chief said.

"Three."

"Do you know them?"

"I've heard them," Charles said.

"Here they are. The three rules. You must agree to them."

"I do."

"You haven't heard them yet."

"I agree to them already."

"One. If found guilty the young men will use ropes to tie your father down to the ground, where he will be beaten."

"I understand."

"I am not finished. He will be beaten until everyone is satisfied that he has had enough. If even one person wants to continue, any person, then it will go on. The only time we do not permit someone to continue beating him is if he has already died."

Charles swallowed. He closed his eyes for a moment. All he could envision was his father face down on the ground with heavy ropes forcing him to lie flat, as thick branches and sticks crashed down on him, ripping the flesh off his body. He opened his eyes, but it did little to help.

"Do you agree with this?"

Charles didn't hear the chief. All he could hear was the cracking sound of his father's bones as the rods made their way through his skin and his muscles and started cracking his spine open, leaving the vulnerable cords inside exposed.

"Do you agree with this?"

Charles looked at his father and then back at the chief. "I agree."

"Two. A bull will be slaughtered in celebration of your father."

Daudi's eyes trailed over to the bull that stood there oblivious to what was going to happen. He found it strange that they would share the same fate. But as Daudi watched the bull he felt regret over his pathetic life. He had done nothing in his days to give anybody joy. And now, in his death, he would finally be giving happiness to people.

"I agree with this."

"Third, the beatings may leave your father a cripple, unable to feed or clothe or take care of himself." Daudi cringed. If ever he wanted a request granted, it would be that he would die instead of being a cripple. Better a dead man than one without his mind, or use of his body, or both, who would be neglected forever. "If death occurs, there can be no objection."

Charles nodded, but the chief did not accept that answer.

"If he dies from the caning, there can be no objection. Do you agree?"

Charles recalled the beatings he had as a child, when his father came home drunk and terrorized the family. He recalled the hours he slaved away at his business to send money home, only to have it wasted on liquor, resulting in more beatings for his mother. And he recalled all the times he told his father to stop.

"I agree."

Esther was not there. This was the way Charles wanted it. No reason to have his wife burdened with the guilt of being present at such an event. Rhoda, however, took her turn to explain, in detail, the horrors she endured. The beatings. How he chased them out of the house. Selling their furniture and animals. Threatening to kill people who wanted to separate him during the fights.

The brothers said nothing. What could they add?

"Charles, we have heard this testimony. Is there anything you want to add?

Charles stepped forward as Rhoda, crying, went back to be with the uncles and aunts.

"I have had it with all the mess. This man has caused nothing but trouble. I've been helping all the time, but nothing is changing. He has not responded to anything or anyone, and now we want the clan to discipline Daudi in order to help the whole family."

Perhaps if this had occurred years later, the courts would have intervened in a better manner. Perhaps there could have been some way to isolate Daudi by locking him in prison until he could be rehabilitated. But this was in the time before there were any courts. The tribal council was the highest officiating body. And if there could be no peace for Rhoda or the children by exhausting all other means, then it was up to the tribe to deal with things.

Permanently.

"Are these accusations correct?"

Daudi cried and said they were true. The chief nodded his head to the young, strong men, who rushed at Daudi and tied him as fast and as tightly as they could. Daudi screamed, as though the realization of the impending torture was now fully in his consciousness. They pushed him down. He tried to get up, but they rammed his face back into the ground. One of them tied a rope around his ankles. Another tied one around his wrists. They took off his shirt and dragged him out under the merciless sun.

His body wriggled like a fish at the end of a line, desperately wanting to be freed. The crowd cheered. Shouting and yelling at the excitement of what they were about to see. Daudi's sweat poured off him. His breathing became erratic. Loud. It almost seemed to drown out the screams of all the others. His eyes grew wide as if to brace himself for the impending beating. Panic filled his face. The cheers grew louder. Anticipation. The blood would be shooting out within the first ten whacks. Even though it sometimes took people an hour to die, they were well on their way after the first ten minutes.

Daudi managed one final look at Charles. Charles looked into his father's eyes and saw something he hadn't seen before. There was something different there. It looked similar to those of the street boys at the burning garbage can—that hopeless glaze in their eyes, that look of utter desperation.

Charles saw a man who was going to die with a lot of sin in his life. His conscience was so plagued by his evil that, even in desperation, he didn't know what good was. Charles heard the deafening screams of the villagers and family members, shouting for him to be beaten to death. For a moment he stepped emotionally out of the picture to see what was going on. He was the only Christian there. That he was sure of. And it made him wonder what kind of gathering this was. They were ready to kill a man for beating his wife. It was justice. But what kind of justice was it?

The first boy took his place as he got ready to begin his turn at slashing Daudi's back. The crowd started clapping. Chanting. An hour later and it would be celebration time with the bull. Daudi looked like a crazed man, his head twitching back and forth, anticipating the horror of the first contact.

Rhoda looked at him and felt the strange combination of pity and relief. Charles stiffened his resolve and watched as the young man waited for the signal. All eyes focused on the chief. He nodded his head.

It was time for the caning to begin.

Chapter 13

The young men yanked back on the ropes, flattening Daudi face down on the ground. He screamed. The crowd shouted in frenzied anticipation. They would have rushed him themselves and beaten him to death with their own bare hands had they not already had the young, strong men there to deliver that punishment. Daudi clenched his teeth and sweat with such intensity that it seemed he had already received the first lash. But that was coming. And when it did, there would be no mistaking it. He thrashed his head from side to side, hoping for some kind of deliverance. But among the crowd he found no sympathizers.

A hundred people crowded around him. Some of them were so close that when the blood would start to fly it would land on them.

Charles swallowed. He wished it were already over. He wished he were back in his car heading home to his wife and family in Eldoret. He wished his father's bloodied corpse were already buried so they could all get back to their lives. But here he was. Waiting. Watching. Wondering. The anxious moments before the first strike seemed like hours. It made him wonder how long the execution would take.

Inside him raged a battle between two convictions: one that knew his father not only deserved to die, but that he also *needed* to die for his mother's sake—and the other one that fought to see that this was still a human being, despised as he was, who was in dire need of help. The tension between the two sides built up in his mind, like two men arguing.

He has to die. It's the only way we can save Mother. He has to go right now. Enough is enough. The decision has been made. The clan has already ruled. They've had their trial, and they've delivered the guilty verdict. Even if you wanted to stop it, you couldn't. The penalty is one cow for interfering by wanting to stop the beating, and even then the clan won't reverse their decision. Leave it be. This is the right course for everyone.

But he's my father. He's my dad. Look at him. So pathetic. So full of sin. Where is he going? Nobody else here understands what will happen to him when he dies. He's only an hour from hell. Something has to be done to stop him.

Charles watched as a young man holding a sturdy stick stepped closer. The crowd breathed a collective sigh of relief and excitement. Finally it was about to start. Finally they were going to get their show. The young man raised his stick in the air. Everything went quiet. It was the silence before the deafening shouts of passion would erupt. Time stood still. It was as if a picture had been taken and they were frozen there. A moment in history. A turning point.

And then it happened.

The stick came crashing down.

Everyone heard the sound of it cutting through the air. It made a sleek, crisp *woosh* as it ripped down towards the target.

Then they heard the sickening crack of wood against flesh. Of executioner against death-row inmate. Of free man against prisoner. Of law keeper against wife beater.

Daudi shrilled. Even though the crowd screamed with vengeance, Daudi's horrible, penetrating yell exceeded them all. He jerked his head back as far as he could and tensed his muscles, as if doing so could somehow dampen the pain. Tears burned out of his lifeless eyes as though something or someone deep inside had already died.

I have to do something. I can't let this go on. He's going to die! He's going to burn in hell! Who's going to help him then? What chance will he have if they kill him? He's going to a Christless eternity. I can't let that happen. I can't let him die.

And what about Mother? What about her? If you step in now, she's the one who will end up dying. How would you like that? How would you like a nice letter in the mail a month or a year from now saying that Mother is dead because Father finally beat her to death—all because your soft, bleeding-heart conscience wanted to be the hero and save this evil man? Forget it. Let him die. This isn't about anger. It's about justice. And you have to decide to stick to your word. How many times have you warned him? You've worked countless hours to give him money that he used for drinking, after which he always turned violent and beat Mother. You've done what you could. You did more than your share. You've done far more than anyone else would have. It's not your fault. It's his. You need to understand that. You're not killing him. The boys with the sticks aren't, either. He's doing it himself. He's finally killed himself.

But he's going to hell. Look at him. He's full of sin. He's horrible. And the only good thing about him is that the evil he causes is limited to this village. He's a man in need of help. I need to help him. I need to step in and stop this. I can't let this go on.

They won't stop, and you know it. It's against the rules. If you step in now, you pay the penalty and they go on beating him anyway. What's done is done. Stop trying to interfere. And stop thinking this is about someone dying. It's not about killing your father. It's about letting your mother live.

This isn't right.

What isn't right? How could this not be right? I'll tell you what isn't right—stepping in now and sealing the misery and likely death of your mother. That's what isn't right.

I have to do something.

Stay where you are.

I have to intervene.

Stay strong for an hour and it will all be over.

Including his life.

Better his than Mother's.

The rod lifted. Daudi looked exhausted after just one stroke. He arched his back in an awkward position to brace himself for the next blow. Hopefully he would be lucky and would get struck in a different spot. A number of strikes in the same location would begin splitting the skin. A few dozen more would expose his spine. And it would only then take a few more to…

"Charles!" Daudi shouted. "Charles, please do something!"

Ignore him. Don't even look at him.

"Please! Charles, I beg you!"

I have to stop this.

Why all this pleading? If you step in now, who's going to help Mother the next time she's getting blow after blow on her disfigured face from this animal? The second strike is coming. That'll shut him up.

"I'm sorry, Charles. Please forgive me!"

He's not sorry. Don't believe him. He's just afraid of the punishment. He doesn't want to end up a cripple. He doesn't want to die. That's understandable. Beating his wife is not.

But look at him. Pleading for help. I have to intervene.
You don't have to do anything more for your father.
"Please, Charles. I beg you. Help me!"
"I can't do anything for you," Charles said. "It's out of my hands."
Good. That's exactly right. It is out of your hands. There is nothing for you or anyone else to do. Let things run their course.
"Please!"
"I have no power," Charles said in an unconvincing tone.
I have to do something. I cannot let this go on.
The young man raised his stick.
Just stay where you are and everything will be fine. Your mother will be safe from now on. Think of your mother. Don't you love her? Don't you want her to be safe? How could you let your mother live under this kind of cruelty any longer? How could you send her back into the hell she is now being released from?
"Stop!"
Charles yelled so loud that it scared the boy holding the stick. Every face turned to him and scowled. Their eyes pierced him like darts.
"Please," Charles said, looking at the chief. "I want to plead with you. I am going to stand for him in the gap. Please do not beat him any more."
It was the first time anyone had ever tried to intervene. The clan looked at each other in surprise and then at Charles.
"Can you repeat what you said?"
"I want you to stop."
Daudi started crying. He closed his eyes as a strong current of helplessness poured out of him. He sobbed into the ground, feeling the relief of knowing that the horrendous odds of having someone intervene had just been delivered.
Charles looked down at his father, seeing a man who never had a mother and who grew up under terrible circumstances. No. That didn't excuse him for who he was or what he had done. It just convinced Charles how awful his father's entire life had been for both himself and for everyone who was unfortunate enough to have had to share it with him.
The chief looked at Daudi and then at Charles. He would fine Charles either way. The question he debated in his mind was whether or not to proceed with the beatings. He saw Rhoda, who was unable to look anyone in the eye. He wondered if she preferred her husband live or die.

The chief instructed the young man to stop beating Daudi. Protests arose from the crowd. Disappointment. Resentment. Anger. They had just been robbed of a good time.

"Can you see what your son is doing for you?" the chief asked Daudi. "He's trying to change the mind of this court."

"I will never do this again! Please!" Daudi said.

The chief penalized Charles one cow for interfering. One cow for one life. It seemed like a good trade to Charles and Daudi. A horrible trade to the rest, save his Aunt Muthikwa, who later revealed to Charles she thought he had made the right choice.

The chief ordered Daudi to be untied and told him to sit down on the ground. They kept him there for half an hour, talking to him and warning him that next time they would not stop the beating. "This is the last time. If you repeat this, we will punish you to death." He told him to stand up, and then he dismissed him. "You should learn from Charles, your son, who took care of the whole family. It's not good that your son looks after your family."

This time when Daudi promised to change, there was a convicted sincerity about it. In that moment when the first stick hit his back, he felt what it was like for his wife when he beat her—to have someone overpower him as he screamed for help.

The crowd left the would-be execution site but had their celebration meal together all the same. There was a sorrowful attitude among them, as though they had paid a lot of money to see an event that didn't deliver the excitement it promised. They gathered where the cow was being slaughtered, leaving Daudi alone as he considered that at this time he could very well have been hearing the snapping of his spinal cord. Instead, he was given a second chance.

Again.

"I have no grudge against you," Charles said to his father. "I am not ready to disown you. But you need to change your behaviour. The beatings, the selling of property, the booze, the mismanagement of money. This will have to stop."

And with that, Charles left his father sitting there in the dirt. He got into his car and began the long drive back to Eldoret. And as he drove, he wondered if the threats would have any lasting impact on his father. Perhaps they would scare him into not committing any of his heinous acts. But either way, it wouldn't resolve the real problem, that inner part of Daudi that was driving him to uncontrolled anger and violence.

Business in Eldoret continued to succeed, while not without its long hours, struggles and difficult decisions. Charles expanded Mullyways to include several more matatus. His grocery store boomed. Everywhere he went he prospered.

Six months after Daudi's near beating, Charles saw a letter on his desk. It was from his Aunt Muthikwa. He sat down in his chair, the same one he sat in to write the letter to the clan, and held the envelope in his hand. Without even opening it, he got an unexplainable feeling telling him that what was inside was going to make him sick. How bad could it be?

He tore it open and read:

> *You must come quickly. Your father is out drinking again. We think he is going back to his old life. Daudi and I have consulted a witch doctor to find out where the problems are coming from. We have discovered that Daudi is being haunted by the evil spirits of the ancestors. The whole family could become like him. Daudi may even get worse. And your business may decrease because of it. Come to Ndalani. The witch doctor will tell us what to do to get the spirits out and get prosperity.*

As Charles read the letter he thought to himself, *there is only one power I know and there is no comparison.* His father had problems, and ones that were too great for him to handle.

It was time for Daudi to become acquainted with the power of the living God.

CHAPTER 14

"Because we *have* to go!" Daudi said.

"Why?" Charles replied.

"To find out why the ancestors are doing this. To find out why this is happening!"

"The drunkenness? The anger?"

"Yes."

"And you think you'll find it there?"

"We will."

"How do you know?"

"What do you mean 'how do I know?' That's where all the important answers come. You know that."

"No they don't."

"They do! Everybody knows this!"

"You actually think going there will help you?"

Daudi's eyes changed from intense to desperate. He wanted to be rid of his burning desire for alcohol. That was certain. He also wanted to be free from the violent acts that resulted from his drunkenness. That was certain as well. But in spite of knowing the damage his drunkenness could cause, his motives for wanting help were far from altruistic. Whatever regret he felt over beating Rhoda was eclipsed by the terror of knowing that should it happen again he would face the clan chief again. For the last time.

He wanted to stop. He *had* to stop. His life depended on it. He had known this ever since the clan gave him that final warning. And he had it all worked out. No booze—no drunkenness. No drunkenness—no violence. No violence—no caning. No caning—no death. It was all so straight forward. But try as he might, Daudi stayed trapped in that unquenchable desire to get drunk. As much as he wanted to, he could not leave it.

He did not possess the ability to free himself from his addictions.

"Yes," Daudi said in a tone that told Charles he did not want to admit the truth. "Because my life depends on it."

Charles looked up at the huge, full clouds that covered the Kenyan sky. He shook his head, then lowered his eyes to look into his father's.

"There is no power there."

"Yes there is! There has to be!" Daudi got that desperate look in his eyes again. "This is the only chance I have."

"It won't help. You'll see that."

"It will! And we're going. We have to go see the witch doctor."

The plan was to leave early the next morning. Charles got up long before his father did. His heart weighed heavy about Daudi's situation. A man in trouble is one thing. A man in trouble who can't get out on his own is another level entirely.

There was no moon. It was so dark outside that Charles had to walk the path by memory rather than by sight. He got to a clearing in the field and knelt down. He closed his eyes and raised his hands.

God, You are all powerful. You are the strongest there is. Your power is far, far beyond the witch doctor.

There was a sudden chill in the air. At first Charles felt it was nothing more than a breeze. But even when the wind passed, that feeling of cold remained.

You know the problems he has. You know—

Definitely. This was much more than just a breeze. A gust of wind calms you down. It cools you. But this was different. Charles swallowed. He wanted to open his eyes and look behind him. But why? What could he possibly see? It was so early. There couldn't be anyone here.

He's fighting an evil spirit. The witch doctor cannot help him. Only You can help him. I pray that Your will and plans will be fulfilled. I pray that You will reveal Yourself to him.

Charles opened his eyes. He turned his head and looked behind him. Nothing was there.

At least nothing that he could see.

They could have taken the car but chose not to, so as to avoid drawing attention to themselves. Instead they walked the seven hours to the witch doctor's estate. It was comprised of six houses. He had three women who stayed with him. And by the look of the hundreds of people sprawled out all over the property, the witch doctor either had the power to help these people or, at the very least, people believed he had the power to help them.

Blacks, Asians, Caucasians, Arabs. Charles and Daudi heard an array of languages as they walked into the crowd. People talked with each other, wondering how long it would take to see him. There was no "first come first serve" system. A person could arrive and be called in right away, ahead of people who had been waiting for hours, perhaps even days.

Charles and Daudi recognized no one. The sick, the addicted, the poor had all come for a cure from the witch doctor.

"Charles," a man said. "You are Charles, and this is Daudi." It wasn't a question. The man spoke as though he was confirming what he already knew.

"Yes," Charles said, studying the man's face. The creepy presence Charles felt while praying that morning returned.

"It is your turn."

"Ours?" Charles asked, trying to jog his memory. "We have just arrived."

"Welcome, Charles," the man said, gesturing with his arm that they should follow him.

They walked with him to the witch doctor's house, passing people who had been waiting for what seemed like forever. They were about to enter when Charles looked back at the man.

"Do I know you?"

"No," the man said, shaking his head. "We've never met. Please, enter."

The hut had a thatched roof, mud walls and floor and a leopard skin on the ground. A small fire burned to one side. There were no windows, so the smoke built up in the room. The hut was in a haze, making them feel they were in a dream.

The witch doctor did not look the way Charles expected. Charles assumed he would find a frail old man sitting in a corner with a pained expression on his face. Instead, he saw a robust middle-aged man wearing a blanket and a cold set of eyes. He just sat there, not saying anything, looking more like a statue than a man. It almost scared Charles when the witch doctor nodded his head to acknowledge their presence.

They sat down across from him on three-legged stools. Daudi looked in anticipation at the witch doctor. But the witch doctor did not look at him.

Instead, he looked at Charles. They made eye contact. At first the witch doctor showed interest in Charles. But the longer they looked at each other through the eerie smoke, Charles began to see the power in the witch doctor's eyes falter to a shaken confidence and then collapse into uncertainty. Fear began to pound in the witch doctor's heart, making it feel like an uncontrollable drum. He swallowed and tried to look away. But somehow, in some way, he was held in Charles' gaze as though forced to do so by some unseen power. He felt he was being electrocuted, a current running through him, terrorizing every cell in his body.

His body began to shake. First it was his fingers. It started with just a twitch. But then it became more intense. His hands rattled back and forth, smashing involuntarily against his body. Charles and Daudi heard a *clack clack clack* sound as his rotting teeth began to chatter. Those eyes. Those dark, hollow eyes of his grew wide, as though they were about to explode. He breathed in erratic spurts. He tried to say something, but whatever he was seeing in Charles' eyes made it impossible for him to utter the slightest word. He stuttered as he tried to break through whatever hold was upon him. Then he managed to speak.

"Why are you here? Why have you come? Why would you do this to me? To us? How can you do this?" That terrible clacking sound came back. His eyes opened even wider, making them look unnatural. He turned to Daudi. "Your son has no problems. Nothing."

Clack. Clack. Clack. The witch doctor's eyes lost focus. They turned a pale yellow in the smoke.

"Go away and come back the day after tomorrow."

Charles did not want to leave. He wanted to hear what the witch doctor would say about Daudi—not for his own sake, but for his father's. He waited for the witch doctor to continue. But all the witch doctor could manage to do was squeeze tears out of those horrid eyes and a whimper, a cry, a plea for them to leave.

Daudi was the first to stand up. He grabbed Charles' arm, hoping for a semblance of reality. Charles stood up, half expecting the pathetic man in front of him to collapse. But he didn't. He just stayed in his chair, shaking, crying, unable to blink those large, petrified eyes.

"Let's go," Charles said.

"Do you see now?" Charles said as they walked back to Ndalani. "Do you finally see now that this man has no power?"

Daudi said nothing. That haunting image of the witch doctor was so real, it was as if he was standing right in front of them.

"When this is all over," Charles said, "you're going to know this man has no power."

After a day of rest they went back for a second visit. They left at 2 a.m. and made the journey to the witch doctor's. The scene hadn't changed. Hundreds sat in groups, hoping their name would be called next. Cows and goats cluttered the walkways as Charles and Daudi came closer. Far in the distance they saw the witch doctor's house. They sat down, wondering if they would be called next.

They weren't called that morning. And as the sun rose high in the sky, Charles assumed they might not get called at all on account of what happened the last time they came. He stood up to stretch his legs, and at that moment, he felt a horrible quiet come over the crowd. People continued to talk, but he heard nothing. A strange silence fell upon him. Daudi said something to him, but he made no reply. He had the feeling something bad was about to happen.

It's nothing, he told himself. *It's just being out in the hot sun. There's nothing to worry about.*

But it wasn't just the sun.

And there was plenty to worry about.

He was about to sit back down again when it happened. He caught it out of the corner of his eye. At first he thought it was just his imagination, that his mind had somehow taken an ordinary event and turned it into something it was not. But when Charles focused to get a better look, he realized he had seen something real.

Fire burst out from the witch doctor's house. It blew the door open. Flames raced out onto the grass and towards the people. The heat and smoke made it impossible for those nearby to breathe. The fire pulverized the witch doctor's house, incinerating him instantly. The flames leapt out at the people like trapped lions escaping from their cages. Panic ripped through the crowd. Screams filled the hot air. People rushed here and there and back again, searching in a frenzy for loved ones.

The fire spread so fast that those nearest the witch doctor's house could not escape. At first, they stood captivated, watching the witch doctor's house burning like an unforgivable firestorm. But what started in fascination ended in terror as the flames engulfed them. The fire ignited their clothes first. Then, as they ran in desperation, their skin began to burn, causing them to scream in agony. Their faces caught fire and their skin boiled. Unable to control their melting muscles, they fell to the ground in helpless balls of red as the flames consumed them.

Charles and Daudi ran back to the road. They stopped only once to see the fire raging in the grass area. The witch doctor's compound was destroyed.

They said nothing for hours. Just the two of them on that lonely walk back to Ndalani. Their steps grinding away on the road was the only sound they heard.

"So?" Charles finally asked. He said it quietly, yet in the silence his word seemed loud.

"So?" Daudi asked, his voice filled with fear.

"Can you see now? Can you see now the God whom I trust is more powerful?"

Daudi did not answer. He didn't have to. He had seen the fire. But that wasn't what convinced him. It was what he saw, or didn't see, in the eyes of that witch doctor. He recognized that look, that helplessness. It was the same look he had in his own eyes.

For years, Daudi had worshipped idols. Now, walking next to his son, he could see that his life was no life at all. Charles had something he didn't.

Charles drove back to Eldoret, feeling the confidence of God's power. Charles took pride in his relationship with God, not because of the inferno destruction but because his father's hope in the witch doctor was broken.

Three months later, Charles was appointed to be a distributor in Eldoret for Total Oil Products. The rate of his business success was much higher than before. It was as though the encounter with the witch doctor had somehow been a catalyst for his endeavours.

A year later, Daudi returned to Eldoret. His drinking had stopped, and this time he was coming not to ask for money but to be with his son.

"You are doing well, my son," Daudi said.

"I have added a sixty-two-passenger bus to my matatus," he said.

"And you are the distributor for…what was it again?"

"Oil products."

Daudi gave Charles a toothless grin. "You've been blessed, my son. You've been blessed."

"Yes."

"God? God has done this for you."

"Yes."

"From where you were? A child with nothing. And now this? God did this for you?

"Yes."

Daudi returned to Ndalani, amazed at how God was able to provide for his son in a way he could not. Despite all the beatings, despite all the abandonment, his son wasn't angry at him. His son had spared his life. Why? Why would he do that?

There was a church in Ndalani that Rhoda often attended. Daudi went one Sunday. And during the service he got up. Everyone stopped. They knew this man. They knew what he had done. The drunkard. The wife-beater. The money-waster. Sure, he hadn't done those things in over a year, but they knew his record. He wasn't Daudi Mulli. He was Charles' father.

"God has been speaking to me," he said.

The church got quiet.

"He has been speaking to me in many ways."

He searched for words. Everyone in the church knew him. Yet he spoke with a sincerity none of them had experienced.

"He has been speaking to me through my son, Charles."

He paused. Public speaking was not his thing. He took in a deep breath and found the courage to look people in the eye as he spoke.

"I've beaten my wife. You know that. I've wasted my son's money. You know that, too." He pressed his lips together, trying hard not to let the tears come out. The weight of all those things—of each time he had hit Rhoda, of each time he had beat one of the children, of each time he had taken the money that was intended to help his children and used it instead to buy booze—hung on him like an impossible load.

"I want my sins to be forgiven."

Charles Mulli in his matatu (taxi) in the early 1970s.

*Charles Mulli in his store taking count of the stock
of his tire and gas business.*

Charles Mulli with some of his biological children.
(From left) Miriam, Charles seated, holding Kaleli,
Grace, Jane, and Ndondo seated, wearing a blue dress.

Charles Mulli as church leader and head of the school board of governor in different schools in 1985. Charles is seated fourth from left.

CHAPTER 15

Charles sat down at his desk. It was the end of another long day, as usual. He had added another arm to his business empire by becoming an insurance broker for cars, worker's compensation and loss due to theft and fire. He had managed to expand Mullyways Agencies Ltd. so that it now included a transportation company, a store for the distribution of gas, tires, grease etc. and an insurance and property management company. The growth was unprecedented in Eldoret. Charles was among the very successful in Kenya. Everything he did turned in his favour.

He looked at the stack of papers in front of him. He sifted through them. A letter from his father. He tore it open.

Son, you have been more of a father to me than I have been to you. You have stood by me when I rejected you. You have helped me when I have harmed you. But I have good news to offer you. I have accepted Jesus Christ. It's hard for me to believe how one decision can change a life, but it has. And I have you to thank. You were right about everything. It's not easy for me to write this. It's hard when I think about who I was. This is why I want to ask your forgiveness for what I did to you. I'm sorry, Charles. I was wrong.

You have been blessed in your life. God has been good to you. You have a good family and you are a good father to your children.

I am proud of you, my son.

Charles stared at the letter. This was unexpected. This was a miracle. Not of the incredible variety. It wasn't a spectacular miracle like a healing or a demonic deliverance. Those would be coming. But for now, this was a changed life. This was a new man. This was evidence that all the prayer, all the forgiveness and all the commitment he had demonstrated to his father had not been in vain.

I am proud of you.

At twenty-nine, Charles was elected to be an elder in an Eldoret church and was also requested to start another church with the help of a British missionary. They started with just three families in a small, worn-out building on a large lot. They focused on the youth, which caused the church to grow at an astonishing rate. They supported the young people's desire to have an English service that was not more than an hour and a half long. They had youth group meetings each week that attracted more and more people. The Mullis were actively involved in the church. Their children sang each Sunday, and Charles either led the service or preached. A few months later he was elected as overseer of eleven churches in Eldoret. The leadership of the denomination loved Charles.

But that would not always be the case.

By 1985, Charles was elected overseer of forty-one churches in a large region outside of Eldoret comprised of more than 100 pastors. Normally, people taking this position needed to be a reverend and have a four-year degree. Charles had neither; still, he was voted in as the youngest overseer ever. He was also elected volunteer chairman of two secondary schools and treasurer of a Christian school.

Soon after, a group of twenty distinguished church leaders invited Charles to join them in visiting Daniel Moi, the president of Kenya. Charles, at thirty-seven the youngest in the group by far, went to Kabarak and drove up the driveway, being watched by guards the entire way. They stepped out of their vehicles, and a presidential aide took them inside. When Moi entered the room, Charles froze. He had seen Moi on TV countless times. He'd read about him in the papers. He respected him. Most everyone in Kenya did. But seeing him in person was something entirely different. He seemed more than just a man, and Charles felt awe in meeting the most powerful person in the country.

Moi spoke with the older members of the delegation, most of whom he knew. Charles stood at the back watching, wondering how it was that he was able to be here. He turned around to speak with another delegate. The two of them spoke about how amazing it was that they were in the same room as President Moi. Suddenly, his friend stopped talking. His eyes looked passed Charles. Someone was coming. Charles followed his gaze.

It was President Moi.

"How are you, young man?" the president asked as he walked by.

The shock of Moi's greeting raced through Charles' body. They made eye contact. "I'm fine," Charles said, not sure if Moi heard him or not as he walked down the hallway and out of sight.

Two months later, Charles and his family received an unexpected visitor at church. Charles' children sang while he sat near the back. Charles never sat at the front. He much preferred sitting with the congregation. Sitting at the front made him feel he would be perceived as putting himself on a higher level than them. So each week he chose to sit among the people to whom he would preach.

People crowded into the new church building, one that Charles helped design, which now had an average Sunday attendance of more than 900. The service was about to begin when a jolt of energy raced through the congregation. People turned around to look at the main entrance behind them. Those still outside watched as a motorcade approached the church. It stopped. Men in suits stepped out and held the door open. President Moi had come to Charles' church.

He walked up the stairs and came to the front of the church as a hush fell over the congregation. He sat down near the front as the service began. He looked around, trying to find someone. Finally, he passed a note to someone nearby: *Where is Charles Mulli?*

A young man came to the back and made eye contact with Charles.

"President Moi wants to see you!" the man said in a half whisper.

Charles swallowed. He walked towards Moi. He saw him sitting with his dignitaries. Why had he come to this church? Why had he called on him? He got to his row, smiled and said hello.

"It's nice to see you again, Charles. I'm glad to be here in your church."

Charles got up to the platform and introduced President Moi, who then came up and addressed the congregation. Charles sat down, and as he listened he felt the amazement and humility of being blessed. He had an incredible family. He had succeeded in business. His church was growing. He travelled from church to church preaching the gospel and saw people surrender their lives to Christ. And now he was being recognized by the president.

Still, life was not without its challenges.

And miracles.

CHAPTER 16

"They're not paying," the deputy chief said.

"That's too bad. Those properties are our responsibility. The rents are long overdue. They're paying, and that's the end of it," Charles said from behind his desk at the office.

The situation had been brewing for a number of weeks, and he had hoped it would have been resolved by now. Charles' company acted as manager for a number of rental properties, including row housing near a slum. The tenants, about forty of them, refused to pay, citing poor excuses for not being able to come up with the money. Charles had sent his deputy chief, along with two security guards and two vans, to resolve the situation, but it did not help. The tenants had banded together, agreeing not to pay.

"But they won't listen," his deputy chief said.

"They have to."

"We've been there for the second time," the deputy chief said. Charles felt the anxiety in his voice. The pressure of another busy day mounted. "But they have formed some kind of a pact—an agreement. Charles, I'm out of options. What can I do?"

"I don't have time to deal with this," Charles said, more to himself than to his deputy chief.

"Please. You're the only one who can solve this."

Charles looked at the clock. He nodded his head. "All right, then. Let's go." He stood up and walked out of the office with his deputy chief. "Bring twenty security guards and six members of staff. Meet me outside in ten minutes. We'll pay them a visit," Charles said, not realizing what he was about to get involved in.

As they drove toward the properties, Charles sensed an uneasiness in his chest. He tried to ignore it, assuming it was the result of having to fit in yet another meeting in an already packed day. He looked out the window. Garbage lay on the street. People cluttered the sides of the road, selling everything from T-shirts to shoes to candy. The longer they drove, the poorer the people became.

The van stopped outside the row-housing units. They got out. Charles assumed the people he had brought with him would be sufficient.

But he would soon find out they were far outnumbered.

A group of twenty tenants walked towards them. One of them ran off to the other houses, presumably to gather the other tenants. And their friends.

"Hello," Charles said, leading his group to the properties.

"We're not paying!" a woman shouted. The groups stopped on either side of the sidewalk as though they were gangs about to start a fight.

"I'm sorry that you're angry," Charles said. "When you moved in you had agreed to pay the rent."

The woman screamed an answer back at him, but he didn't hear it. His attention was diverted to a group of people gathering around the tenants. He looked to his left and then to his right. He saw still more people from the village and slum coming, seemingly out of nowhere, to surround them. Within moments, 300 people surrounded them and dwarfed Charles' delegation of less than thirty persons. That feeling of panic in his chest came back—as though the earlier attack was some kind of warning that Charles realized now he should have heeded.

"We are refusing to pay!" another man said. "We don't want to see you. We will never pay. We must fight you!"

While they had no argument and no just cause for their action against Charles, they definitely had numbers. Ten to one. That spoke volumes.

Charles wanted to leave. This was pointless. Even if they called the police, they would not get there in time if this turned unruly.

It was getting dark. And the disappearing light brought with it a heightened sense of uncertainty. The sun faded along with Charles' chances for a peaceful resolution. He had come with the intention of convincing his tenants to pay the rent. Then his priority shifted to resolving this without any trouble. But now he was at the point where he just wanted to get out.

Alive.

He was about to tell them he was going to leave when he heard a horrible scream coming from somewhere in the crowd. What horrified him was not the sound of the voice but what was being said.

"We are going to burn you!"

A jolt of terror ripped through Charles' team. The crowd screamed in agreement.

"Bring a tire and fuel and burn them!"

As if killing someone wasn't bad enough, slums often found extreme ways of executing people. One of their methods was to put a tire over the heads of their victims, down to their waists, pinning their hands inside. They would be beaten, doused in gasoline and then set on fire. The crowd would watch and cheer (similar to how villagers would cheer when caning sentences were carried out) while the smell of burning flesh filled the air. They would shout insults as the sound of a dying person's screams faded from a horrific roar to a muffled desperation for air and a once healthy body was reduced to charred bones and flesh.

The moment that cry rang out from the crowd, the threat of dying became very real to each team member.

God. God, what do You want me to do? I thought I could solve this. I thought I could come down here and make things right. I thought I could help. We're in trouble, God. We are in very, very serious trouble. It's out of my hands, God. They want to kill us. And You know they will.

Charles swallowed. The crowd came closer.

"*Mnangonjea nini?*" someone in the crowd shouted, meaning "what are you waiting for?"

"*Choma! Choma!*" they screamed, meaning "burn them!"

Charles' heart pounded with such force it reminded him of his days as a child when he lay awake on his bed at night and heard his drunken father coming into their hut. He looked at the people. Many of them were drunk on *changa'a*, an illegal, alcoholic homebrew. Adrenaline raced through his body with such ferocity that it felt as though someone were sucking the blood right out of him.

God? God, what do I do? God, they're going to kill us!

The crowd came closer. That horrendous chant *Choma! Choma! Choma!* drowned out every thought he had.

The sun set. The crowd's fierce eyes came nearer. The deputy chief shouted as loudly as he could. "Listen to me! People, listen to me!" But it did nothing. Not a thing. The screams just got louder. More intense. They shouted with such rage that it rang in Charles' ears.

God, we are in a very, very difficult situation. You see what's happening here. Now save us from these people. Cover us with the blood of Jesus Christ.

In that instant Charles felt a sudden boldness and courage. It was as though he had just been fed a powerful intravenous drug that eradicated his fear and gave him a whole new power. *Why should I be afraid of these people? Who are they to scare me?*

Charles broke through the people around him and jumped on top of a truck. Everyone looked up at him, especially the people from his company, who felt their lives were now resting on whatever he did or did not say.

"People!" he shouted. The crowd became still. They were like a raging sea that turns to glass in an instant. It was a shock to all those who were there. From a dreadful frenzy to an unexplainable peaceful calm. "We did not come here to make war. I came here to solve the problems and conflict." Nobody moved. They had become as one person. "I want to tell you there is nothing more to talk about." Charles felt an incredible confidence in Christ. Something he never felt before. Not in this way.

The strength in the crowd drained. Their overpowering numbers suddenly felt insignificant to them. It was as though fire was about to proceed from Charles' mouth and consume each one of them right there on their properties. They waited, fearing the worst, for what Charles would say next.

"I tell you in the name of Jesus Christ to disperse!"

Immediately, they ran in all directions, with such intensity it was as if wild lions had suddenly been let loose on them. Within seconds, they were gone. Escaping into their houses. Retreating into the slum. Seeking refuge away from this man with the unknown power speaking from on top of a truck.

Charles stood there looking at his employees, who stared up at him in utter amazement. Some of them had their mouths open. Some were more frightened of him than they were of the crowd. Charles got down from the truck. They got into their vehicles and drove off.

Thank You, God, he prayed. *You delivered us. You have delivered us.*

The following day, Charles sat down at the same desk he had been sitting at when his deputy chief walked in the night before. He pulled out the file on the properties and got the list of addresses. He wrote letters to each of the tenants, explaining what was required of them.

And each tenant paid the required amount in full.

CHAPTER 17

Charles Mulli was about to have the kind of day people have when something ordinary happens that in retrospect becomes the catalyst for a whole new life. For some people, it's meeting that special someone for the first time in an apparently chance encounter. For other people, it's opening their e-mail or a letter to discover they've been accepted at some university or received the job they wanted.

For Charles, it started with a routine trip to Nairobi.

He drove down Kenyata Avenue looking for a parking spot close to the Nyayo House building where he needed to update the registration on his buses. It was mid-morning and most of the spots had already been taken. Up ahead he noticed street boys standing on the side of the road. Eight of them. Seventeen to twenty-two years old. Dressed in dark clothes. Dirty faces. They waved at him, trying to show him they wanted to help him find a spot. Charles slowed down and followed their lead. They ran ahead and directed him to where he should go. Sure enough. An empty spot. Charles parked his car and got out.

"Give us a shilling," one of the boys said.

"Just one shilling. That is all we ask," another said. "For helping you."

"We will watch your car for you. We will take care of it."

Charles wanted to help them. And why not? They'd helped him. But the look in their eyes, the desperation and addiction to glue/gas sniffing, told him that whatever money he gave them would be spent on hurting themselves. In the short run, a high on sniffing glue would dull the pain of their upbringing (or lack thereof) and give their minds a break from living in their rotten existence, if only for a short while. But when the effect of the drugs wore off, they'd be left to search for another man looking for another parking spot from whom they could get another shilling and start the whole thing over again.

"I'm sorry," Charles said, realizing he was late but still wanting to help the boys.

"We helped you. We helped you find a parking spot."

They stank, too. It was an awful combination of body odour, glue and gasoline. It was hard for Charles to take in. They crowded around him, holding out their hands, begging for a chance to escape this world, if only for a short while.

Food. He could buy them food. He looked around as he walked, but could not see a store. There probably was one nearby, but the entourage of beggars surrounding him made it difficult for him to see anything beyond the hopeless sets of eyes gathered around him.

He pushed past them into the building.

A half hour later he came out, having renewed his licenses. He walked down the street, and when he got to where he thought he had parked his car he saw an empty stall. He walked back in the direction of the building, thinking maybe he had gone too far. Still nothing. He turned the other way and walked back with that sinking feeling people have when they think their car has either been towed or stolen.

Up ahead he saw one of the street boys who had begged him for a shilling. He was tall. Strong. Very, very strong. He wore an oily and torn shirt with an old cardigan.

"Have you seen my vehicle?" Charles asked.

The boy did not reply. Not at first. He looked back at Charles with a vengeful look on his face, almost seeming to be glad to see him again.

"Have you seen my vehicle?" Charles asked again.

"Did you employ me to be your watchman?"

The boy looked away from Charles and said nothing more.

Charles went to the nearby office of a cousin to phone Esther and tell her what had happened. Then he and his cousin drove to the police station to inquire if they knew something. An officer told them no car matching the description had been reported. He took a statement from Charles. "Once the vehicle is found we will let you know," he said.

But no one would ever find out what happened to Charles' car.

Charles sat at the back of a crowded bus on the way home to Eldoret. He hadn't taken public transportation since he began his business driving his matatu. Like every other bus leaving Nairobi, there was always room for one more person. People jammed in beside him, making six people fit onto a bench that should have seated four. But the crammed bus wasn't on Charles' mind. Even his stolen car wasn't troubling his thoughts as he rode home on the dusty road in the sweltering heat.

He was wondering about those boys he had turned down.

The look in their eyes. Desperate. Absolute hopelessness. Bordering on panic. *Why are they on the street? Why doesn't anyone look after them? Where are their parents? What happened to both parents, that these boys have no home?*

Their disgusting clothes and putrid smell stayed with Charles. Rancid odour filled his memory. *How could they get so dirty? Where do they sleep at night? What do they do when they don't have any food?*

He'd forgotten about the car. He'd forgotten about the pressures of his business. That morning when he had arrived in Nairobi, his mind had been filled with problems he had to solve. Now, on the way back, he was preoccupied, even consumed, with trying to understand how these street kids got to where they were.

Whose fault is it that these boys are on the street? Is it their parents' fault? Maybe they had negligent parents. Maybe their parents just aban-doned them. Charles could relate. *But all of them? Do they all have such terrible parents? Or maybe a father died of AIDS and the mother worked as a prostitute and couldn't afford to take care of her kids, forcing them to scrape out whatever existence they could begging on the streets.*

Maybe it was the government's fault. Not enough programs to help these kids. Not enough time or money being invested in group homes to help them get back into society to contribute in a meaningful way. But the problem was so vast. Street kids were just part of the out-of-con-trol poverty epidemic in Kenya. Hundreds of thousands of people living on less than a dollar a day in slums all over Nairobi, not to mention other parts of Kenya, or Africa, or the world.

Why? Why are they on the street?

The bus stopped. Charles didn't move. *Why are they on the street?* People left the bus. They had arrived in Eldoret. *Who is going to help them?*

"Eldoret," the bus driver said.

What happens to them? Do they stay on the street their whole lives? Who gets them off the street?

The last few passengers left the bus, save Charles, who sat at the back still preoccupied with those street boys—the dirty, stinking street boys without food, without shelter, without a future.

Without hope.

"Eldoret!" the bus driver shouted.

Charles looked up from the window. The bus was empty.

He gathered his briefcase and got up from his seat, his back sore from sitting in the same position too long. He walked off the bus.

Who gets them off the street?

It was late. His family was asleep. Charles stood outside looking at the stars that filled the night sky from horizon to horizon. There was a cool breeze blowing. It was a perfect evening. Charles should have felt calm. But instead he had a heaviness in his heart he could not ignore.

It had been three years since his car was stolen. The burden for street children was planted in his heart that day, and it had kept on growing in intensity to the point where it was now causing him sleepless nights.

He had often helped people by giving them money for school or buying them food. He was generous with everything God had given him. Still, the feeling of needing, of having, to do something more tangible for the street children kept pounding at his heart's door.

What can I do? This problem is enormous. What can I possibly do? How can I help?

There was a struggle inside of him. Part of him wanted to help the street children; part of him wanted to be content with the luxurious life he had.

I've got to help them. I've got to do something. Me. I have to do it. The government is doing what they can. The parents of these children did what they could. Who knows what has happened to them. But now I have to respond. I have to get involved. God, I need to be involved.

Wait. Wait. Now think this through. Don't do anything stupid. You've worked hard for yourself and your family. You have important friends. You have an incredible business. If you do something foolish now, you will be jeopardizing your entire family. Is that what you want? You want to put them at risk? Go back inside the house. Look at your children. Look at your wife. They need your money. They need your attention. What right is it of yours to neglect your own children to help those on the street? Keep sending money to people in need. But don't go overboard. Why should you? Someone else will be there to take care of them.

But I have to do it. It's on my heart. I can't let it go. It's a calling. I know it is. Deep down inside I know this is where I am supposed to be. I can't explain it. I just know that I know. Isn't that what I am responsible for? For being obedient to what God has called me to do?

Has God called you to do this? Did He really say you were supposed to do this? Is He really calling you to go into the streets, of all places, and help these children? All you have is this gut feeling. This intuition.

But I know it's right.

Right for whom? For them, or for your wife and children? You're doing so much as it is. You are so generous. You are giving more money than anyone could possibly expect you to give. If you do something extreme to help these kids, like giving up your businesses, how long will it last? You'll lose all your money, and then what? Who will support you? You will become a burden to other people. Who will look after your wife and children? Think of what might happen to them when the money runs out. You will have destroyed their future. Who will pay for their schooling? For their clothing? For their opportunities? How fair is that? You will turn them against you for being such a fool so as to help those street children and deny your own.

But how can I fail if I follow the calling God has placed on my life? Will God lead me into financial destitution? If I do this, will He let me down? How can a man possibly fail if he follows God?

There are too many street children. Have you counted how many there are in Eldoret alone? Thousands. And Nairobi? Thousands more. How can anything you do make a real difference? How can anything you do matter in the grand scope of this vast poverty problem?

It will matter to the people I help.

"Again?" Esther asked, coming outside to join her husband. She smiled, hoping to bring some relief to him.

"I have to do something," he said.

She stood beside him, feeling the pride wives feel when they have husbands they admire. "I don't know what you're planning, baba Kaleli." She used the term *baba Kaleli* in keeping with their tradition that wives do not call their husbands by their first name, but by the name of their first son.

"Then don't feel bad," Charles said. "Because I'm not sure what I'm planning either."

She let out a quiet laugh and made eye contact with him. "You're probably the only person in all of Nairobi who gets up at night to think about the street children. Do you know that?"

"It's a start."

"A start? A start for what?"

"I...I don't know. Not yet. But I will. I can feel it. I'm going to know very soon."

They stayed there in the quiet for a while, feeling the cool breeze as it blew on their faces, beside them and around them, filling the entire yard.

"I'm with you, Charles. You know that."

"I do," he said.

He hugged her, and she went back to bed.

Charles looked up again. *God, I need to be sure this is of You. I've never been to the inner city for evangelism, God. I don't even know what to do. And who is going to run my business? All those impoverished children. They can become important people, God. They can become what You designed them to be. Look at what You did with me. Thrown out. Rejected. My education only goes to grade eight, and look what You've done for me. If You've done it for me, then why not for them? But they need someone. Someone has to help them.*

He began to cry. His success in business was a dream for any Kenyan—and for most people around the world. And yet, there was no longer peace about the work he was doing. Yes, he was serving God through the church by preaching, and he was involved in supporting numerous ministries. But there was so much more out there. Something was missing. And Charles believed beyond any doubt that it lay in helping the street children. It wasn't something he could explain, yet it was impossible to ignore.

God, I need discernment. Your discernment. About what I should be doing. Do I continue with business, or do I go to help the street children? You will direct me, God. I pray Your guidance, in Jesus Christ's name.

Charles opened his eyes. He felt the weight of decision-making on his shoulders.

How can I help them? What about my business? Who would run it? What will happen to my family? Will I be jeopardizing my children's future? Which way do I choose?

Charles prayed. But the uneasiness did not leave him. So many questions. So little peace. So little confidence about the direction to take.

But all of that would change on November 17, 1989.

CHAPTER 18

Charles felt like vomiting. His stomach hurt. His head pounded. His body pumped out sweat. Everything felt wrong. Dizziness. Disorientation. Fatigue. He drank a glass of water. It did nothing to help him. He sat back in his chair at his office, taking deep breaths and tried to relax. It wasn't malaria. Maybe a flu? He closed his eyes, hoping the feeling would pass, thinking that if he shut the world out for a while things might return to normal and he could get back to work. He felt a momentary relief from his pain and assumed he would be able to carry on with his day as usual.

But little did he know what was about to take place.

He stood up from his desk. He felt uneasy. It was as though he was on a ship getting seasick. He put his hand down on the desk to steady himself. This wasn't a flu. This was something different. Something entirely new.

"I…" he said to his secretary as he walked down the hallway and passed her desk to the door. She could tell he wasn't right. The normally upbeat and positive Charles had been replaced with a man burdened by too many things to smile at her on his way out.

"Mr. Mulli?" she asked.

"I'm going."

"When do you plan on coming back?"

"I'll be gone for the rest of the day," he said, turning to her and giving the best smile he could manage given the circumstances. "I'm going home."

So he thought.

He got into his Mercedes Benz and put the car in drive. He felt a sudden tiredness again, similar to the way he felt after working those three straight days driving the matatu. That dizziness came back. Exhaustion. This wasn't just an illness. There was something else to it. *Why do I feel so awful?* He stopped at the parking lot exit and waited for an opening to get on the street. He took in another deep breath, closed his eyes and tried to relax.

The next thing he knew he was driving on the highway. The shock of finding himself there made him grip the steering wheel, as if doing so could give him a tangible way of holding on to reality. He looked ahead, down the road he was travelling on. Then he looked to each side. This wasn't the way to his house. *Where was he? And how did he get here?* He glanced at the rear-view mirror and then out the front. Nothing looked familiar. He looked at his watch. He had been driving for half an hour.

None of which he remembered.

He saw a sign in the distance. He was in Turbo. He blinked. *Turbo? Is that what the sign said?* He looked closer just as it went by. Sure enough. Turbo.

Charles was on the way to Uganda. Nowhere near home.

He pulled over to the side of the road and stopped the car. His heart began to pound again. *What happened to the last half hour?* It was a blank. No record of it. It was as though he had vanished and someone else had taken his place.

Suppose I would have hit a bus or a trailer while I was driving. What would have happened? I could have killed them. I could have died.

A tear came to his eye. He tried to make sense of what was happening to him. And then, in a burst of emotion, tears streamed out of him. For three hours he stayed there. Crying. Thinking about his life. About his decision.

Do I stay in business, or do I leave it all and help the street children? I need to make a choice today. Here. Now. Either I pick up this vision and put it into a mission or I say no to it and move on.

He closed his mouth, thinking that he was about to throw up. That aching feeling in his head came back. The tears soaked down on to his shirt.

I need to decide. Which way do I go, God?

But instead of hearing God's voice, he felt a horrendous tension inside of him. Two forces clashed, like some massive tug-of-war with one side pulling him to stay in business and the other side pulling him to help the street children.

Look at what this is doing to you! This is crazy! All this talk of giving up your business and turning your back on how God has blessed you. You've made yourself sick. You're hallucinating. You just about died on this highway. Driving around, not knowing what you're doing. You're killing yourself, do you understand that? You and you alone are driving yourself mad by wanting to give all this up. Can't you see what a danger you've become to yourself?

But this is my mission. I can feel it. I can sense it. How can I turn my back on what God is calling me to do? He led me out of poverty. He lifted me out of my fate as a destitute child and made me into a success story. I have nothing in my life, not one thing, where I am failing. Everything I have touched has succeeded. So why would God call me to leave that? Why do I have this unrest?

Because God is not calling you anywhere, that's why. If God really was calling you to do this, why would you be feeling such unrest, such illness? Where is this infamous shalom—*this peace of God? It's not there, because God is not in this decision.*

He has to be. I'm following Him day and night. He wouldn't have given me this passion unless He had a plan. He wouldn't put this dream of helping children inside me unless He wanted it to develop.

If He wanted you to do this He would not have taken you down this path in life. The path you are on is the best path a person could possibly have. Think of how much you are doing for the poor. If you give your money away, what can you do for them then? You can do nothing except ride down to the depths with them and drag your family down with you. Then you will look like a fool. Your political and business connections will be lost, and you will be a disgrace, not only to God and to your family but to yourself as well. You will end up where you started—a beggar on the streets. Your decision to leave what God has given you will show people what it means to turn their back on God.

But God took me on this path for a reason. I was an orphan. I was at the bottom. I was trampled down. And look at me now. I have a purpose. I have a relationship with Jesus Christ. I have a life that matters.

This is why you should stay.

No, this is why I should go.

Go?

Nobody understands these children better than I do. When other people see these children, they see lost causes. But I don't. When other people see them, they see thieves and prostitutes and drug dealers and beggars. But I don't. I see…

What? What could you possibly see in them?

I see…

You see what?

I see myself.

Everything went still. The many late nights he had stood under the stars unable to sleep began to make sense to him. The undeniable feeling he had in his spirit since the day his car was stolen became clear to him. The passion for helping children fell into place.

Yourself?

This is not about my life. It's about theirs. It's not about how Christ has blessed me; it's about how Christ can use me to bless them. They have gifts like I do. They can have a future just like I do. I can only reach so many. But if the people I reach in turn reach others…isn't that the point? Isn't that what I'm being called to do?

You've lost it. And you're only going to have yourself to blame.

I'm no longer listening to you.

You're going to listen. And you're going to turn this car around and go back to work. The poor need money.

They need me.

They need your financial resources.

They need the love of God through me.

They need to get themselves out of that mess!

They need me to lead them out! And that's final! That's final!

His body trembled. Tears ran with such intensity that they distorted his vision. The pain in his body grew worse, making him feel he was about to explode.

"God," he called out. "Here I am. Tell me what You want with my life."

Healing raced through his body. He stopped sweating. The uneasiness in his stomach disappeared. He felt no pain. Instead of agony, he felt a sudden peace. It was as though someone had switched his life from chaos to order. From uncertainty to confidence.

Even though cars raced by him, he felt a strange stillness at the road side.

"God, show me. Here I am, Lord. I'm ready to move by faith and to be used of You. I'm ready to give all that I've been holding in me. God, use me."

The struggle disappeared. The air felt cleaner. He looked at the gorgeous trees with their full leaves that he somehow hadn't noticed when he pulled over. A rush of power went through him.

This is it. This is the decision. I'm leaving the business world, and I'm going to help the street children.

The burden of how to provide for his family was lifted. The shackles of worry were replaced with freedom. He laughed, sitting in his car. Then he sang a hymn with the confidence that people walking with God have when they make the decision to give up everything to follow Him.

Thank You, Lord. I will be with You on this journey. And You will be with me. I will serve only You. I will do my best.

He drove over the nearby bridge, turned around, crossed over it again and headed home to Eldoret to share the news with his wife and family.

"You are home too early," Esther said as Charles entered the house. She was busy getting her things together to go to the market and was only half-interested in Charles' response. He paused. It should have relayed to Esther that his reason for coming home early was more than what she would have anticipated. Charles nodded his head. This was it. He had to tell her.

"It's been an interesting day," Charles said, searching for the right words.

"Well, what is it?" she asked. Charles searched for words. She kissed him on the cheek. "We'll talk about it when I get back," she said with a smile. She put her hand on his forehead. "You are feeling all right?" She looked at him more closely. "Baba Kaleli, are you feeling all right?"

Will she get angry? Will she feel as though her entire world has been pulled out from underneath her? Will she be supportive? I know she wants to stand beside me, but this is the most a man can ask of his wife. How will she react?

He looked at her and felt the uncertainty men feel when they are in the presence of the woman they love and are hoping that what is about to happen will keep things that way.

She smiled again. "Charles. You look so…" she studied his face, his eyes. "You look so…I haven't seen this look before." She stopped smiling. Her inquisitive nature was replaced by a deep sense of awe. There was something in his eyes. Something different. Something engaging.

Something powerful.

"We'll talk about it when I get back," she said again in a whisper, watching his eyes, wondering what was going on behind them.

She turned and walked out of the house.

The Mulli family gathered for supper. Charles sat at the head. He gave thanks for the food. They began eating. The children talked back and forth about school, about girls, about boys, about football. It was a normal Mulli supper.

For now.

"I have an announcement to make," Charles said. A sudden silence filled the room. It was as though they had all become statues, fixing their gaze on Charles, knowing subconsciously that the words he was about to speak would change their lives forever.

Charles cleared his throat. They stayed locked on his face, looking for a hint of what was about to come. There was something in his eyes. Thinking back on it later, they had noticed it when they came home that day. There was something in his eyes then. That, coupled with him having come home earlier that day, should have sent a signal to them. But sitting at the supper table now, looking at his eyes again, told them that whatever was on his mind and in his heart was about to impact their lives as much as it had already impacted his.

Esther studied him as well. There was something different about him. The young man she saw for the first time while working in the pineapple fields now had an entirely different look.

"We have been blessed in this family," he said as he looked at each of them. "But being blessed is not the chief aim in life. I can work hard to give you a bigger house and bigger cars and long vacations, but is that really what we are all about? We serve God in this family. And when God leads us in a different way, we are presented with a choice to either follow Him or go back to what we had before."

They could all feel it coming. This wasn't going to be an announcement about starting yet another business or about moving to a new house. This was going to be serious. This was going to be big. Regime change.

"For years, as you know, I have had a burden for street children."

Those two words were their first clue. They wondered if this was good or bad. Street children. Street children. Street children. It echoed in their minds as an indication of what was to come.

"I was abandoned as a child. And now that I'm older, seeing abandoned children does something inside me that I have not been able to ignore. I've searched. I've prayed. For years. And yet there has been no clear answer. Not until today. A man can not ignore his calling. He can try. But it will never leave him. And if he doesn't follow it, he becomes something less than what God wanted him to be. And so I have made a decision. It's a decision that will affect us as a family."

Affect was the operative word. The real question on all of their minds was *by how much?* They waited in silence. Charles breathed in and took a moment before delivering the words that would not only impact them but countless others as well.

"I've decided to sell all the businesses and commit my life to helping the street children."

CHAPTER 19

Silence can be deafening. The Mulli children could tell you why. After Charles made his announcement, no one said a word or gave any indication of how they felt. No cheer. No sagging shoulders of despair. Just silence. Now that his course of action was out in the open, they had a chance to think it over, wondering how this was going to change not only Charles' life but their own as well. *Help the street children? How? Do we all get involved? Why do we have to sell the businesses to help them?* They would have begun questioning his decision had they not sensed the conviction with which he had spoken those words.

The longer they waited, the more uncertain Charles felt. The initial shock of the news had come and gone. And they felt collectively more awkward with every passing moment. But salvation came by way of the oldest daughter, Jane.

"We'll be praying for you, Dad," she said, breaking the state of disbelief into which he had put them.

Her words brought life back to the table.

"That's quite a change," Esther whispered. The way she said that made Charles wonder whether she was in favour of the move.

"It is," he said, trying unsuccessfully to make eye contact with her.

And then things reverted to being quiet again. Everyone had a chance to absorb the weight of the decision. Some would have a delayed reaction. But for the rest, the question of how this decision would change their lives began to set down upon them.

"How can he do this to us?" Jane said with enough force to let Grace know she was both worried and angry about what was going to happen. She closed the door behind her and paced up and down the room while her sister sat on the bed. "Do you know what this means? Do you have any idea? What is the matter with him?"

Grace said nothing. She didn't have to. She was thinking the same thing as her sister.

"And why didn't he ask us first? And why *all* the businesses? Why not just spend some of his time doing it? Half and half. But everything?"

Grace tried to process what was happening. The announcement wasn't the problem. The problem was the uncertainty of her future, which was now put in jeopardy because of what their father had said.

"And schooling? Think about that. Where is the money going to come from? And what happens when we sell the businesses? What do we live off?" Jane asked, pausing for a moment. "Where does he get this from? Did God really tell him this? Would God put us at risk like this?" Her tone of voice changed from curiosity to frustration to desperation. There was no recourse. There was no changing their father's mind. They all knew that. It felt as though they had gotten on the wrong train and were heading in a direction they never expected.

Or wanted.

"And what about our friends?" Jane asked. "When we no longer have the nice cars, the nice clothes, the nice things in life. You think they'll talk to us then?" She stopped as a wave of anxiety gripped her. "Will we still have friends?"

Jane sat down and buried her face in her hands, as if doing so could shut the world out, if even for a moment, and she could return to the life she had only a few hours earlier. She shook her head, hoping to wish away the reality that had just been created for her, wanting instead to find herself in the relief sleepers feel when they wake up to discover their distress was just a dream.

She looked at Grace, who stared straight ahead. Her lack of words was evidence that something was at work inside of her. "Grace?" Jane asked. "Grace, what are you thinking?"

"I'm scared," she said.

"Me too."

"Everything?" Esther asked, coming out to the backyard to see Charles under the night sky. The kids were asleep. She had picked her moment carefully. No need to cause dissension among the family.

"It's the right thing, Esther," Charles said. He held out his hand to motion her to stand beside him. But she hesitated, conveying this was a decision she neither expected nor supported.

"Are you able to separate yourself from your money? Your house? Your family?"

Your family? Charles turned his head to look at her worried face. "This isn't about separating me from my family, Esther. I would never…I could never do that. Not you. Not the children. Not ever."

He was sure about this decision. That was the trouble with men like Charles. When they had made up their minds there was no discussion. No turning back. And this time, it was more intense than ever.

"And you've thought about how you will support us? You have a plan for how we will live without money? You've spent time organizing this decision before springing it on us like this?"

Charles didn't have an answer. *We will trust the Lord* just didn't seem to fit right now. He didn't have a plan. But in spite of everything his business had taught him, he didn't need one. Not now. Not in advance. He didn't need to see the future laid out in order for him to take the first step. The confidence of Christ in him had gotten him through that. But now the challenge of the future lay before them. And while Charles believed that what lay ahead was far superior to what would become of them if they stayed on their current path, he could see that this passion, understandably, had not been transferred to his wife.

Not yet.

"But you're behind me, aren't you?" Charles asked, with a hint of worry in his voice.

"Baba Kaleli, what are you doing? Your whole business? Everything you've worked for? Don't you remember where you came from? Who you were? Do you want to go back there?"

"This is why I have to do this. Not for us. For them."

"They are more important than us?" It wasn't a question. She had drawn a line and was standing toe to toe with her husband, looking for a definitive answer on whether street children whom he did not know had risen in importance in his life over his family whom he did know.

"Of course not."

"Yet you are willing to do more for them than you are for us."

"It's not like that."

"Then what is it like, baba Kaleli? What is it like?"

She deserved an answer. On everything. She had a right to know. She had a right to be confident in the path down which her husband was taking her. It was just that things were a little difficult to explain. If only he could reach inside and give her the assurance he had in his spirit that while things didn't make sense on one level, they made perfect sense at the highest level.

"Are you with me, Esther?" he asked.

She looked up at the stars. Only a few days ago they were standing in this same spot looking at the same mysterious holes in the universe. Then she had felt the conviction women feel when they know they are a team with their husband. But now, that feeling was replaced, not with animosity but with doubt—which is sometimes just as bad.

"Esther," he said again. "Are you with me?"

Charles went up to his bed thinking about the voice of the Lord he had heard that afternoon. Esther was asleep. And as he lay down, it occurred to him that while they were so close they had never seemed further apart.

I am not a very special man, God. I am like any other person. You know this is the hardest decision of my life. And yet, I am not worried. Why is that, God? Why is it that everything in my life is about to change, yet I don't feel any panic or anxiety?

We'll start planning tomorrow. You and I. We'll start making a plan for how to help the street children. The ones who have been thrown away. You will rescue them.

But God, I also want to pray for my family. They are my responsibility. You know that. And You know their hearts. You have called me. You have called us. You are faithful.

I wonder what tomorrow will be like.

The next morning began like any other. Charles was the first to get up. Esther prepared breakfast for the family. The children got up. The older ones got ready for school. Everything looked the same.

But it felt different.

It felt different for all of them. That looming question hung over them. How much? How much would this decision affect them? Breakfast was quiet. Charles said goodbye to Jane, Grace, Miriam, Ndondo, Kaleli and Mueni as they left the house. Esther cleaned up breakfast as Isaac and Dickson went into a nearby room to play.

"So this is the first day," Charles said with a smile.

"That's right," Esther said, not looking up from her work.

"I'm going to be upstairs. Planning. You know. How to close the businesses."

Esther nodded as a sign that she heard, not that she agreed.

"I'll be heading out this afternoon. To the street. For the first time," Charles said with an undeniable excitement in his voice.

Another nod.

"I'll see you at lunch?"

Charles waited but got no response.

By noon, Charles had succeeded in laying out his exit strategy for the businesses. He thought it strange how he spent years building everything up and only a few short hours giving it away.

Charles then worked on his strategy for reaching the children. The streets and the schools were the best places to minister to them. Children without food or shelter or God would be in the streets. Because the children in the schools likely had enough food and shelter, the focus there would be evangelism. He sketched out more details. And when he had finished laying out a plan, he put down his pen and stood up from his desk.

It was time to go to the streets.

On the afternoon of November 19, Charles drove down the streets in the poorer areas of Eldoret, looking for children in need of help. It wasn't hard. They were everywhere. Dirty clothes. Dirty faces. Desperation in their eyes. He stopped his truck. A group of five boys stood on one side of the street, looking at him with suspicious expressions. Three girls on the other side of the street gave him the same look.

Charles got out. He smiled. He stretched out his hands palm up and gave his own customized greeting. "*Ooo-aye*," he said. It was neither Swahili nor English. Just some greeting he made up to identify himself for the children. The children made no response. Charles reached into the back of his truck, where he had packed bread, milk and sodas. He pulled them out.

This the children understood.

"Would you like something to eat? Come, join me."

Their desire to eat overshadowed their apprehension. Their first few steps were cautious. Their focus on the food never wavered. *Why is he doing this? What does he want from us?*

"My name is Mulli," Charles said. "Here, this is for you." He broke the bread into smaller pieces for them. Their dirty hands reached out and accepted it from him. They stuffed it into their starving mouths, and before the first handful was swallowed they were already reaching for more. Hand after hand reached into his pile of bread until it was exhausted.

They looked up at him, wondering if there was any more. Their eyes looked different. There was something in them that wasn't there earlier. The beginning of hope, perhaps.

"Of course!" Charles said with a smile. "We have more bread."

He got out another loaf, and in moments it was devoured. He laughed as they ate. The children did, too. Their mouths filled to overflowing, they giggled as they jammed more into their famished bodies.

Charles reached into the back of his truck. He poured milk into cups and gave one to each of the children.

"This is for you," Charles said. After they finished drinking the milk, they nodded their heads and gave a quick *assante*.

"Would you like to hear some stories?" Charles asked.

The children looked at each other as if to determine what his motives were.

"Why do you want to tell us stories?" one of them asked.

"Because I want to tell you that Jesus loves you."

"Jesus?"

"Yes, Jesus."

"He loves us?"

"Exactly," Charles said with a smile.

"You want to tell us stories about Jesus who loves us?"

"That's right," Charles said, his voice showing the assurance that he believed they were about to join him. "And I'll have food, too. It's not that far. We can go right now...unless you have other plans for today. If you can't come, I understand."

"We don't have any other plans."

Charles did not hear them. "Because if you can't make it—"

"We'll come," they said. "We can come right now."

"That's great," Charles said. First contact a success. "Thank you for coming."

They walked to the church that Charles and the British missionary had started. They sat down in the field, drinking soda, eating bread and telling stories. Charles spoke about Jesus, who lived a perfect life and died so they could have a relationship with God. They listened to him until late in the evening.

"What can I do for you?" Charles asked them. A hush fell over them. They felt the wind around them pick up.

"For us?" the boy replied.

"Yes. What do you need? I can bring you food again tomorrow, and I can tell more stories and even teach you some songs. But I want to help you. What can I do?"

They told him they also needed clothes and a place to sleep.

"I will figure something out," Charles said. "It may take some time, but we will come up with a solution for you."

They took more bread as they left the church property and thanked Charles, the man who had come out of nowhere to help them, the forgotten street children. One of the boys stopped and came back to Charles.

"Yes," Charles said.

"Could I ask you a question?"

"Of course."

"Why are you doing this?"

"Giving you food?"

"The food, the stories, inviting us to come back. Why? Why do you do this for us?"

"Because Jesus loves you."

"And you?"

"I love you, too."

"You don't even know me."

"I don't have to know you to love you," Charles said.

"Does Jesus love me the way you do?"

"He loves you more."

And those words stayed with the boy all night.

CHAPTER 20

Charles continued building rapport with the street children by giving them food and clothing. Most of them came to the church to spend time listening to his stories about the man named Jesus and saw the relationship between God up in heaven who loved them and Charles Mulli on earth who showed it.

They played sports like football and volleyball on the church grounds. They had their bread, milk and soda lunch together. Part of the problem with the street children was that their stomachs weren't able to handle solid food, so Charles had to gradually wean them off of survival mode and get them started on a daily diet. He asked Esther to help him by providing meals for the children.

"I want you to meet the children," he said.

It had been two weeks since Charles started his new mission, giving Esther the time she needed to take in the enormity of the change. She struggled between two lives—the one she knew as a mother and a wife to a successful businessman, and the other that she knew nothing about.

She nodded her head.

"Perhaps you could cook something for them?"

She nodded again.

"Thank you," he said. "The children will love that. They will really love what you will cook for them."

Esther went to the kitchen to prepare her first meal for the street children. That afternoon Charles took Esther and introduced her to them. They looked so ill. So tired. So unclean. So abandoned. They needed something to eat. They needed someone to clean their clothes. They needed a place to sleep.

They needed a mother.

She watched in silence as the children ate her food. It was a desperate sort of eating, not the calm, relaxed pace that comes to people who know there will be another meal. They thanked her and went off with Charles. She cleaned up what was left and watched as Charles left with them to play a game. As she returned to her home, she wondered what it would be like to be alone. To be on the street.

To be without family.

Two months later there were thirty children coming to the church grounds each day. Esther always brought food, and with the food came the opportunity to get to know the children. She began to counsel some of the girls, who were struggling to be free from working as prostitutes. At first, it was horrific to hear their stories about the lives they were trying to escape. But the longer she listened, the more she found she had a desire to help them. A desire to make a difference.

A desire to be part of rebuilding them.

Charles developed a one-acre farm on the church property so the children could learn to plant cabbages, carrots, onions and tomatoes to feed themselves. The boys slept in a small building on the church property, a welcome change from having to sleep outside in the rain and cold. Each day Charles played games with them, taught them songs and told them stories about Christ.

"We can't bring them into the house," Esther said to Charles as they stood together on the side of the field watching the children play football. They ranged in age from seven to twenty, all of them playing together as friends, almost as though they were brothers and sisters.

"Do we send them back to the street?" Charles asked, wishing there was a way to take them all home and protect them from the drugs, gangs, prostitution and violence of the streets. "There are so many. So many."

"I can't let these…" her voice trailed off. She saw the young girls running to get the ball and realized they were only hours away from nightfall, when some of them would likely be involved in other activities. "I can't let these girls go back into the streets." She covered her mouth. "We have to do something. We can't take them all. But we can certainly take some."

"We can take in three tonight," Charles said. "I think that will work."

"Yes. We will take three." She looked at the children. "But which three? How do we decide who gets to come and who has to go back to the street?"

After saying a prayer they chose a seven-year-old boy named Wanjohi and two girls, named Susan Wanjiku and Washeke.

They brought the three children home that evening. It was the first time a street child entered the Mulli house. They came in through the door and entered a brand new world.

Charles' biological children came downstairs to meet them, their new brother and sisters.

"Hello," Kaleli said, being brave enough to break the ice.

The new arrivals said nothing. They had never seen a house like Charles', much less been inside one. And they'd never been in a family with eight children.

"These are your new friends," Charles said to the three newcomers. "These are my children."

He introduced them to his biological family and then took them upstairs to their bedrooms. The upstairs rooms had been rearranged so that those children who once had their own rooms were now going to share a room with a sibling.

At bedtime, Charles tucked in the three new additions to his family.

"We are living here with you now?" Susan asked.

"Yes. This is your new home."

"Do I get to stay here tomorrow?"

"Yes, Susan. Tomorrow you will be here as well."

"When do I have to leave?"

"You don't have to leave. This is where you will stay."

"I like it here," she said. "This is better. I feel safe here, Mr. Mulli."

"I'm glad you feel that way. And you don't need to call me Mr. Mulli any more. You can call me Daddy."

That was new. That was very different for Susan.

"All right. You're my new daddy?"

"Yes, Susan. And I am very, very proud to be your daddy."

He kissed her goodnight, turned off the light and closed the door.

"What are you doing?" she asked with enough force in her voice that it told Esther she thought all this was insane. "Giving your money away? Why don't you stop your husband?"

Esther stood outside under the evening sky with a business friend. They had known each other a long time through their husbands who had worked together.

"We're helping them," Esther said. It came out sounding more like an admission of defeat than a proclamation of doing something good.

"You think this is the right thing to do? To give away everything you and your husband have worked for?"

"It's important for the children."

"Which ones? Yours, or the ones in the street?"

Esther took in a deep breath and tried to calm herself down. She was ready to tell her friend that she, too, thought it was a mistake. That everything Charles was doing was crazy. What kind of a path were they on now?

She had been here before with other business friends, trying to explain to them what they were doing and why they were doing it. But none of their friends understood. Week after week they saw their social network of contacts crumble away. The Mullis had been rejected by their friends as though they had a contagious disease. Now, Esther's last friend had come to pay her a visit.

But it felt more like a warning: Change your ways or we're through.

"The street children are important, too," Esther said.

"You don't believe that, and you know it. You've been doing this for two months now? You know your situation at the bank. How much longer can you do this? A year? Two years at the most? And then you'll be just like them. You'll be asking me for help."

Esther felt ill. She knew everything her friend said was true. Depending on how many children they took in, they could be bankrupt by the end of next year. And then what? Who would look after them? What would become of her family when the money ran out and the children went back to the streets?

"You are the one who has to convince Charles to drop it," she said. "You are the one who has to show him that what he is doing is wrong."

Easier said than done, Esther thought. She wanted to confide in her friend that she wasn't happy about this. No. Not just unhappy. She was more than unhappy about it. She was worried. Stark fear. She and Charles knew what it was like to be on the bottom. *Why would we climb our way out of that only to volunteer ourselves to go back in?*

"It really has been nice seeing you," her friend said. "I've got to get going."

"We'll get together again soon," Esther said, wanting to give a courteous goodbye. But instead it came out feeling like more of a question, as if deep down she realized this might be the last time they saw each other.

Her friend hesitated. The normal response would have been *of course we'll see you soon*, but her silence spoke volumes. And Esther felt disappointment, knowing their friendship was based on financial status. Nothing more.

"Goodbye," her friend finally managed as she walked down the driveway to her car. She backed away and left without waving. Esther heard the car drive off. She turned around, walked passed Charles and went back inside to be a mother to yet three more children.

"We have to sell off more of the businesses," Charles said.

"Then sell them off." Esther washed a pot, rinsed it and placed it beside the growing stack of plates.

"We will be selling the last farm."

"No," she said, cleaning an unending stream of cutlery. "You are the one who will be selling it." She regretted that. She regretted how it came out. She wished she hadn't said it and continued with the dishes.

Charles waited until he thought the time was right. "It's the one with the oranges, bananas, vegetables and the springs. You know the one."

"Yes, I do. I was the one who planted it with you."

"I wanted you to know before we gave it away."

"When does it end? Or do you continue to give it away until..." Her voice was raised. It was late. He was glad the children were asleep. The house was at full capacity after taking on more children, including Nduku, also called Faith, a five-year-old girl with an irresistible smile.

This is what we need to do," he said.

Esther stopped everything. Her body seemed to collapse against the sink. She hung on to it as though it was the only thing keeping her from falling to the ground. Something deep inside her welled up, and she began to cry. Charles both saw and felt her pain. He walked to her and put his arm around her. She sensed the tension between staying at his side and leaving. "You are ruining us," she whispered.

Her hands began to tremble. It was as if she felt a struggle to maintain her fragile grip on her old life.

"I'm not forcing you on this path," he assured her. "I can only say that I know we are going in the right direction."

"This is not easy. These children. They are not easy."

"I agree."

"They are not what I expected."

"You don't like this?"

She pressed her lips together. "Don't like this? Don't like this?" She looked at him with a tired expression, trying to find the confidence in his eyes that could pull her from her world of doubt to his of belief. "What's not to like? Our children are berated at school. They are laughed at. Their future is in jeopardy. Our friends are gone. Our money is gone." She shook her head. "Do you hear me?" She spoke so quietly that Charles had to watch her lips to make sense of what she was saying. "Are you listening to me or are you so caught up in your grand and impossible vision of reaching out to street children that you have lost your mind?"

"I am listening to you."

"We are out of resources." She bit her lip and closed her eyes, feeling the horrendous weight mothers feel when they sense the insecurity of the prospect of not being able to provide for their children.

"I know this is where God wants me—where He wants us. I know that I know. He will look after us. Please believe."

She turned back to the dishes, hoping the soothing touch of water would somehow calm her down.

"I'm trying. Right since the very beginning. I'm trying to believe. But there are kids in my house who don't listen. They break things and don't care. I know some of them are stealing from us. From our own home. They are stealing from us. I have no control any more. I'm at the end."

"So was I. I was at the end. And I found out that this is where it begins."

"At the end?"

"Yes. When we realize we have no recourse, we know it will be all up to God."

"This is my point. Will He come through? When the money is gone, will He abandon us?"

"No."

"Will God abandon our children?"

"No."

"How can you be so sure? How can you see down the road and know how it is going to turn out?"

"I can't. And I don't have to."

"Why?"

"Because I have God's promise. I know what He has told me to do."

She turned back to the dishes and looked up at the evening sky. She remembered the day when she first met Charles and thought it remarkable how her life changed with that one encounter. She remembered the day he started his business. She remembered the feeling of being free from poverty. Of being secure in a stable financial situation. Of having family, friends and a future.

And then she wondered if by giving up her life she might be able to provide that same hope to others.

"Do you think they will change?"

"The children?"

"Do you?"

"I think we're going to find out."

She nodded her head. She could still hear her business friend's voice saying goodbye as she drove off. Then, in another room, she heard crying coming from one of the street children.

One of *her* children.

"I need to see what's wrong," she said, walking past him to the room.

"Are you with me in this?" Charles asked.

Goodbye friends. Goodbye money. Goodbye prestige.

"I am with you," she said.

Street children filled the church yard. Fifty kids ran around playing games and laughing. Some of them played football. Some of the girls braided each other's hair. Charles sat with the younger children, joking with them, throwing a ball back and forth. He stood up from his game.

"*Ooo-aye!*" Charles shouted.

The younger children echoed back. "*Ooo-aye!*"

It took a second time for the ones playing football to realize he was calling them to come together.

"*Ooo-aye!*" he shouted again.

"*Ooo-aye!*" the kids replied. They all gathered around him.

"We have had a good day today," Charles said. "We have had fun playing games and singing songs and telling stories." The kids clapped. "Who wants to sing another song?" They all cheered. "Who wants to sing another song?" They cheered louder. "Who wants to sing another song?" They stood up on their feet, clapping and cheering. One of the boys stayed on the ground and turned over a pail. He grabbed a nearby stick and began banging a drum beat on the base of the pail. The children began swaying back and forth with the rhythm. They clapped their hands. Charles laughed as he joined them in clapping. It was his job to lead them in a song. But he suddenly lost the ability to do so. It was something he saw in their eyes. It was something he felt in the way they were clapping. He clenched his teeth, trying to fight off tears. He nodded to a girl in the front row who then came up and led them in a song.

Nimegundua siri	*I have found a secret*
Nimegundua siri	*I have found a secret*
Nimegundua siri	*I have found a secret*
Ya kukaa ndani ya yesu	*And it is in Jesus.*

The singing was unlike anything he had heard in any of his church choirs. All of these children came from unchurched backgrounds, yet their singing had such a passionate and honest quality that it made Charles wonder why it sounded so different. He listened as the group of children managed to sing loud enough to attract attention from people on the sidewalk at the far end of the church property.

Charles looked at the small army of children. Prostitutes. Addicts. Thieves. Gang members. And here they were now, praising God instead. A few of them were already showing signs of being freed from their problems. Many of them would leave this place tonight and go right back to their struggles. But there was time to change them. There would be opportunities for them to be healed. At least for now they were here, where God wanted them.

And Charles was where God wanted him, too.

Tembea tembea	*If I walk and walk*
Zunguka zunguka	*If I turn around and turn around*
Inama Inama	*If I bend down and bend down*
Yesu ndiye bwana	*Jesus is still the LORD.*

Charles' attention was diverted to a number of cars gathering on the church lot. One car after another found parking spots near the front door. Men wearing suits stepped out and walked into the church. Charles recognized them. They were elders and other leaders of the church. He wondered what they were doing here. He was on the board. If it was a meeting, he should have been invited. He assumed it must be a last-minute thing. Sure enough. One of them was on his way over to meet him.

"Hello," Charles said, stretching out his hand.

The man only nodded. He tried to block out the singing.

"We are having a meeting," the man said. "We would like you to come."

"We're almost done."

"The meeting is now."

"I'll be there when we're done."

"The elders have come. The pastors have come."

"Then I'll be there right after the children are gone and the young boys who are staying at the small house on the church property have gone in for the evening."

The man cringed when he heard that. "Charles, come now. They are meeting about you."

Charles stopped clapping. He had had a feeling this might be coming. For months, people from the church had been avoiding him. Brushing past him. Not speaking with him after services. At first he thought nothing of it, but over the course of weeks he noticed people were not as friendly, not as open to him. Some had come right out and asked what he was doing with the street children. That was to be expected. They just needed some reassurance about the need to help these children.

"We're almost done," Charles repeated.

"We are expecting you now," he said again and walked toward the church.

But Charles did not leave. He sang with them until they were done.

"That was incredible singing," Charles said. "You have really touched my heart today with how you sang and how you worked in the field and how you are all playing so nicely with each other. I love you very, very much. You are so special to me. All of you. And God loves you, too. When you leave this place and until you come back tomorrow, I can't be with you, but God will love you."

The children became quiet. The restlessness left them. Things became quiet on that church field.

"Charles!" the man shouted from the church door.

Charles didn't look, though the children were distracted by what happened. They turned their heads, wondering what was going on.

"All of you know that God loves you," he said. The quietness returned. The children looked back at him. "And some of you here today don't know Jesus yet. You know that Jesus died on the cross for you and that He rose again from the dead because He wants to give you a new life and forgive you for everything you have done. He wants to make you into a new person and lead you in a new life.

"Some of you do not have parents, but God will be your new Father. Some of you don't have many friends, but Jesus will be your very own special Friend. Some of you have bad memories of what you did and what other people did to you. Jesus will live inside you. He will clean your minds. And He will bring forgiveness into your life for the things you have done to others and the things others have done to you."

The elder at the door could not hear what Charles was saying. In frustration he opened it and went inside.

"Jesus said 'I have come to give you life and to give you so much that it is overflowing.' This is what God wants to give you. So who of you tonight would like to give their life to Jesus Christ and follow Him?"

Half the children raised their hands. It blew Charles away. Here he was in an open field in Eldoret speaking to street children, some of whom he had only met this day, and already they wanted to start their journey with Jesus Christ.

He led them in a prayer and encouraged them to come back the next day—not that he needed to. He was the only show in town that handed out free food. They would need little persuasion.

After the children left, he walked to the church. He went inside and found the room where they were having the meeting. The moment he opened the door, the talking stopped. The room became silent. The *who's who* of the church were all there. Elders, preachers, university lecturers, ministry heads, businessmen. They crowded around a large table with their hands folded as though striking some kind of a deal. Some of them looked up at him and then turned away, waiting for someone else to formally greet him. After an embarrassing silence, one of the elders stood up and gave a smile that looked to Charles like it was forced.

"Sit down, Charles," he said, motioning to a chair.

Silence. Again. Charles tried to understand why. They all knew each other. They'd been friends for years. Still, he felt as though he was meeting them for the very first time, as though they were all strangers even though their faces looked familiar. He sensed the chill that comes when optimism is replaced with an undeniable feeling that what you thought would be a friendly get-together is instead turning out to be something much more.

"Hello," Charles said, almost wanting instead to give an enthusiastic *Ooo-aye* greeting. He sat down on an unstable chair at the end of the table. "How are all of you?"

A few nods. No real answers. They avoided eye contact. The elder in charge continued.

"We want to talk with you, Charles."

"Great," Charles said. "I want to talk with you, too. We are having a great time with the children. They are laughing and playing and learning about Christ. And tonight, praise the Lord—and I mean that—some of them got saved. Street children have given their lives to Christ."

The room turned to ice. Their faces to stone. One of them clenched his jaw. An uneasiness crept into the room. It felt as though the men in front of him had somehow been hypnotized or reprogrammed. Normally happy people, the group closest to him appeared both worried and angry. There was trouble brewing. There was something at stake. There was something wrong.

Charles looked the elder in the eye, and what he saw concerned him. There was no fire behind those shells. There was no compassion. They seemed hollow to Charles. Empty.

"We do not approve of what you are doing," the elder said. "We are instructing you to get rid of the street children."

CHAPTER 21

No one moved. They stayed there in silence. The air felt heavy—like a massive weight on their shoulders. At least the news was out now. It was official. There had been many secret meetings behind his back, many late-night sessions to discuss how and when they would tell him. All of that was now behind them. They had managed to give him the message. Those sickening children. Those repulsive robbers, prostitutes, thieves and gang members polluting the church grounds with their filthy presence. They would corrupt the good children of the congregation. They would mooch off the hard-earned tithe of the parishioners. They would get a free ride and drag the upstanding members down with them.

What right did they have to be on their property? What right did Charles have to infiltrate the church with these people?

"Get rid of them?" Charles asked, hoping he had heard wrong. But he hadn't, and deep down inside he knew better. He had noticed their lack of involvement, their lack of encouragement and their lack of interest in supporting his ministry with the children. They had been avoiding him for months. Now he knew why.

"They have to go," the elder replied.

Charles crossed his eyebrows. All of them and just one of him. He looked around the table at sombre faces. They were jurors who had just delivered him a guilty verdict.

"Why?"

The tension got worse. Charles felt that one of them was about to begin shouting at him. Some of them pressed their lips together. They weren't interested in a dialogue. *We don't want those kids. Get rid of them. The meeting is over.*

"Charles, we've discussed it," the elder said.

"Discussed what? Casting the poor back out into the street?"

"That's not the point."

"Then what is the point?"

"Charles."

"Look at you. Elders. Preachers. Businessmen. Tell me why you want to throw them back on the street."

"It's not right," one of them said.

Charles couldn't tell who said it, but whoever it was may as well have been speaking for the whole group.

"I've been here since the church started," Charles said. "We have grown from three families to over 1,800 members. I wasn't wrong then, was I? How can you say I'm wrong now?"

"Charles!" one of the businessmen to his left said with enough power that it convinced everyone this meeting was not about having a debate. He breathed in and tried to regain what little composure he had left. "You are bringing street children onto the church property. Prostitutes. Do you hear that? Whores from the street. What will happen to our children? Have you considered this? They will learn their ways. They will become like them."

"I'm sorry you believe that," Charles said.

"I'm sorry you don't."

The elder spoke in as even a tone as he could manage. "Charles, we can't have this."

"I'm not looking for your money," Charles replied. And the moment he said that the group seemed to have lost some of its ammunition. "I'm looking to help them. Orphans. Outcasts. I understand them. I was one of them. And now I've been called by Jesus to help them. By Jesus Himself. Who exactly are you to tell me to stop?"

"Don't challenge us on our decision!" the elder demanded, his face becoming angrier. Perspiration formed on his forehead. This was supposed to be quick and simple. In and out. Not some debate. And certainly not some debacle where they would be told they were disobeying Jesus by removing the poor. "The membership is behind us. At least 95 per cent."

They stayed in a stalemate, neither party sure of how to convince the other of how right they were. Charles prayed silently, looking for wisdom, looking for help, looking for resolution.

"When I was younger I asked God, '*What did I do to deserve this kind of life?*' I never got an answer. I never found out. But God raised me up. Right from the very bottom. And now I see these children—mirror images of me—walking down the street wondering who they are, where they come from, where they are going, what will happen to them, whether there is any hope. I wonder: *what did they do to deserve their life?* I don't know the answer to that. But I do know that God has called me to help them."

No one knew what to say. The elder in charge felt the most pressure to respond.

"We are all trying to follow God's calling on our lives. But how do we know if God has truly called us to certain things? How can we say that we are honouring God by putting the church at risk, especially the youth?"

"Unless we say, '*Yes, here I am,*' we can't be used of God."

The real problem wasn't about the youth anyway. This was about class. Charles saw it in their eyes. This wasn't about protecting children. It was about protecting ego. It wasn't about being God-fearing. It was about being religious. It was about prestige. Appearance. Position. Image. And if Charles was involved in helping the poor, the addicted and the sick—and if they condoned it—then maybe, just maybe, that might mean they would have to get involved with the street children as well.

Heaven forbid.

"I think you've heard our decision," the elder said. And this time all of them looked at Charles. Those sets of eyes glared at him with a unifying stare of excommunication.

Banishment.

Charles swallowed. What was there to say?

He sat there. Stunned. Not fifteen minutes ago he was talking with street children who had just given their lives to Christ. They were happy. They had hope. They had the first inklings of a future beyond the street. And yet now, Charles was staring at angry faces belonging to people who knew God.

To some degree.

Charles nodded. He closed his eyes a moment as if doing so could somehow erase the reality of what was happening. He stood up, turned around and walked to the door. He was about to leave when he turned back for one final look at the group. Very few looked up at him. Charles opened the door.

He left.

CHAPTER 22

It had only been two and half years since Charles started the ministry, but already he had managed to exhaust his fortune. Esther saw the day coming. The number of children continued to grow, as did the expenses. Finally, he sold the last orchard, marking the end of self-sufficiency. The well was dry. It was as if he never had any money in the first place.

It was quiet in the living room. Late. Charles stood beside his wife, who was sewing a patch onto an old pair of pants. Two years ago she would have thrown them out without hesitation and bought a new pair. But not now. Now, every spare pair of pants mattered.

"That's it?" she asked. "That's really the end?"

"It is." Saying, or admitting, it out loud felt like a revelation for Charles. It was as though it was now clear he was now devoid of any personal resources to rescue himself.

"Are you worried now?" she asked.

"No."

"No?"

Charles looked at her and shook his head. "Why should I be worried?"

"Because there is no money, baba Kaleli," Esther said.

"God owns the cattle on a thousand hills. He will provide for us."

Esther put the pants down. Anxiety gripped her. She struggled to believe, feeling the tension people face when deciding how to navigate through the stormy ocean of faith. "Do you really know that? Or are you just saying it because you think it's what I expect you to say?"

"You'll see, Esther. We didn't get called into this to be humiliated. Humbled, yes. Humiliated, no."

She looked at him with eyes that needed every reassurance he could offer that they had made the right decision in going this direction. He moved closer beside her and put his arm around her.

"I've never regretted this decision." He looked at her. "It isn't boring, is it?" It caught her off guard. She was unable to respond. Charles smiled. "This is the edge. This is real life. The burden on us it too much to bear. That's how we know we're in the right place. Don't be afraid. God has to provide. We have no other hope."

Word had spread throughout Eldoret that Charles was not only taking in street children but he was also praying for the sick. In 1992, he came home from a meeting at six o'clock, and Esther told him people from the hospital wanted him to pray for the patients.

Taking with him a team of three others, Charles went to the Uasingishu hospital. It was dark when they emerged from the shadows into the light shining from the main entrance. Charles led the way and introduced himself to the nurse at the front desk. She seemed relieved when he walked in. It was as if his presence alone had a calming effect on her.

"I'm glad you've come." She didn't look well. Exhausted from worry. "We have so many sick. We can't help them. I've heard that you pray for people and they are healed. Is that true? Have people actually been healed from illnesses?"

"Where can I pray for the patients?" Charles asked.

"We have three wards," she said. "Thirty people in each ward. The patients have malaria, typhoid, some have been injured in accidents..." Her voice trailed off as she tried to jog her memory. There were more illnesses plaguing the patients. She had dealt with some of those other illnesses that very day, yet she was unable to recall what they were. She felt the strain of a long day in her neck muscles. "One has already died. Today. This morning. Many more will die soon. We have given them the proper medication, but it hasn't helped. They're not getting better."

"Lead me to them," Charles said.

She stood up and blinked a number of times to bring what temporary relief she could to her dry eyes, realizing only then how sore they were. She took them down a hallway to the first corridor. She stopped and turned to Charles. "Will it work?"

"My prayers?"

"Yes."

"It will help. To what extent, I don't know."

"But how can you not know?"

Charles gave a brief smile and then returned to the gravity of the situation that surrounded them. "I don't have to know. I'm not supposed to know. I'm supposed to be obedient. That's why I'm here. This is why I've come. That's why you've called me. I've come at your request to pray for the sick to be healed of their illnesses."

Charles opened the door to the first room. The moment he touched the handle, his knuckles felt sore. It was as if a momentary attack of arthritis had gripped him. He stretched out his fingers and walked into the room. There were four children lying on beds. Two on either side of the small room. They looked at him, wondering who he was and what he was doing here.

"*Ooo-aye*," Charles whispered. His quiet voice broke the eerie silence in the room. His voice had managed to bring a welcome relief to their situation. The children said nothing. Their eyes never left him, watching him as he walked into the middle of the room.

"I've come to pray for you," he said. "I know you are sick." The moment he spoke, the feeling he had only moments earlier in his hands suddenly gripped all of his joints. His ankles, his knees, his hips, his shoulders, his elbows. They ached with such intensity that it seemed as though someone had stuck needles into him and was injecting him with a debilitating drug.

"And I know that the doctors are doing everything they can. They are working very hard for you."

The pain got worse. He felt their physical pain and their despair, worry and fear as well. He felt the horror of their uncertainty.

"But I believe in Jesus," he said. "I believe that He died for us to make us whole. He can make us better. I am here to pray for you to be delivered from your sickness."

One of the children looked at the others, trying to determine if what she heard was correct. Healed? Of typhoid? Does that happen? Do people get healed of diseases that kill?

He went to each of their beds, laying his hand on their heads, praying a simple prayer for Jesus to heal them. When he was finished he left, seeing no change in their condition.

He continued with his team, visiting each patient in the hospital. Person by person he laid his hands on them, rebuking the illness and praying for a touch of God to come and restore them.

As he was leaving, the nurse followed after him. "Did it work? How do you know that it worked? They are not better. Shouldn't they be healed?"

"I've done what I can." Charles didn't know what else to say. He didn't know what else to do.

"What happens now?" she asked. In her tired face he saw her desire to convey some kind of hope to the patients. "Do they die? Do they live? What do I tell them?"

"We will continue to pray and wait and see."

It was the afternoon of the following day when Charles got word the hospital wanted him to return. He and his team came to the entrance. Things were calmer than normal for this time of day in the hospital. Nothing moved. Nothing was going on. He walked inside. He saw no one. No doctors. No nurses.

No patients.

Behind him, he heard footsteps. Running towards him. A familiar voice shouted at him.

"Mulli!" He turned around. "Mulli!"

It was the tired nurse. Only she had somehow found an incredible burst of energy. She stopped in front of him, trying to catch her breath.

"How?" she asked. "How did you do it?"

Charles shook his head. "Where is everyone?"

"The doctors have confirmed it. They've confirmed each one."

Her eyes were wide now. She stared at him with amazement, the way people stare at a famous actor or singer.

"Confirmed what?"

A tear came to her eye. Then she smiled. "It's empty. The hospital is empty."

"Empty," Charles whispered, sensing her astonishment.

"They've been healed," she said. "The patients aren't here any more."

CHAPTER 23

In spite of growing expenditures and the mounting pressure to feed and clothe the street children under his care, the burden to evangelize only grew stronger in Charles. He planted several churches. He also spoke at schools and churches throughout Eldoret, at least in those that would tolerate his message. He often travelled to other parts of Kenya to preach the love and power of Jesus Christ with the same conviction of the minister years ago when he had been saved at a youth rally.

"Where is this school again?" Esther asked as she got on board the bus. At the back of the bus a children's choir from Mully Children's Family (MCF) practised the songs they were about to sing for the service. A team from overseas was also with them. Like other teams who had come to MCF from all over the world, they had come to teach the children and reach out to those in the slums.

"Lugulu," Charles said as he and his wife sat down. The bus started off. The children clapped. The team joined them in the song. The sun was shining. It was a perfect day.

"Are you all right?" Esther asked, noticing a tinge of uneasiness in her husband.

He nodded. "I'm fine. Thank you. I'm fine." He smiled at her and held her hand. And yet, he was unable to shake the feeling of uncertainty. Preaching always came at the expense of battling the attacks of the enemy. He recognized the feeling—that uncertainty of something waiting in the shadows for an opportune time to strike.

They travelled to western Kenya, driving down a highway filled with potholes. They slowed down each time they passed through a small town. Crowds of people ran out from the side of the road or from under their small umbrellas, carrying papaya, bananas, pineapple slices or soda drinks in glass bottles. They hurried to the windows, pushing their products into the hands of the passengers, especially the white people, hoping for a chance to turn their meagre merchandise into currency.

When they finally made it to Lugulu School, they saw five girls standing in a line waiting to greet them. Other students had gathered behind them to get a look at the visitors. Huge cheers went up. They clapped as the bus turned onto the parking lot and came to a stop.

Charles stepped off the bus, followed by the children. He greeted one of the teachers and then proceeded down the line. He shook the first girl's hand and asked her name. He smiled and thanked her for coming. Then he proceeded down the rest of the line. When he reached the last girl, he stretched out his hand. She hesitated a moment as if unsure of what she was supposed to do. She raised her hand. Charles smiled. He stretched out his hand to touch her. Just as he was about to make contact, her body suddenly shut off. It was as if the life in her had vanished. She stood there as a corpse and then collapsed to the ground like a dead person.

The other girls screamed. Students ran off in every direction. Panic broke loose. Charles felt the weight of evil in the air. He bent down to look at the girl. She was breathing.

They carried her to a first aid room and laid her down on a bed. Some of the MCF children crowded around Charles to see if they could help.

"What is this?" one of the teachers asked. "This girl is healthy. She has no problems. What's going on with her?"

Charles stood beside the girl. He rested his hand on her forehead and prayed. "Jesus, this is the work of the devil. There are 1,200 girls here at this school. This has happened so that people would not listen to Your word. I'm asking that You would intervene. Let this girl stand up and be delivered."

The team prayed for twenty minutes, pleading with Jesus to set the girl free. "Lord," Charles continued. "You know the devil wants to hinder these students from accepting the Holy Spirit." At that moment the girl sat up as though being woken from sleep.

"Praise God!" Mulli and the others shouted.

She looked around the room, trying to figure out how she got there. "What happened?" Charles asked.

"I can only remember the moment you came. I can't remember anything more until this moment."

Charles took her by the hand. "In the name of Jesus Christ, stand up!"

She stood up. Everyone started singing and clapping. Shouts of joy went up. They left the first aid room with the girl restored to perfect health.

They went to the assembly area in a dining hall, where all 1,200 girls and the teachers had gathered to hear them. As they entered, their singing brought a determined interest to the students who only half an hour before had run off in a frenzy. The team began by giving their testimonies and then performed a skit about Jesus' parable of the wise and foolish man. The MCF choir, made up of twenty students and Mr. Mulwa, a longstanding teacher, sang for them.

Charles came to the front and preached about the salvation of Jesus Christ and His love to humankind. As the students listened from their dining tables, Charles quoted Revelation 3:20:

Behold, I stand at the door and knock; if any one hears my voice and opens the door, I will come in to him and eat with him, and he with me.

It was so quiet in that hall that each word he spoke echoed from the sheet metal roof. He paused. "Jesus died on the cross for your sins. There's nothing you can do to be rid of the bad things you have done in your life. The Bible says that you were even born into sin. And you can't be free on your own. You need Jesus Christ as your personal Saviour. He loves you. No matter what kind of family you come from, no matter what kind of background you have, Jesus loves you.

"If you want to give your life to Jesus Christ, I'm going to ask you to come forward. If you hear His voice, don't delay. Come. Come forward to surrender your life to Jesus Christ."

And they came.

Over 300.

They left their seats and their old lives behind them and came forward to receive Jesus Christ into their lives.

The ride back in the bus was quiet. Most of the MCF children and the team were in awe—amazed, yet not surprised—at what had happened. Charles sat in the front with Esther, thinking about the deliverance and the hundreds who got saved. It occurred to him that had he hung on to his businesses, this opportunity would have slipped away into eternity. Had he not left everything behind and followed Jesus on that November day four years ago, no one on this bus would have been to Lugulu school.

Three hundred.

Charles smiled. "Thank You, God," he whispered. "You've really done something here today."

*Charles at the highway location where he decided
to follow God's call to help street children.*

*Children after a rescue mission. Charles took them to
Two Rivers Dam where the children took a shower.
He preached the Word of God to them and fed them.
Afterwards, they did some exercises.*

Charles with some of his biological family members. (Left to right)
Mueni, Grace, Charles, Isaac, Ndondo, Esther, Kaleli, Dickson.

Charles Mulli.

CHAPTER 24

"You're going to be late, Dad," Miriam said.

"I know. I know. But I had to see you girls again," Charles said with a smile. He reached out and gave Jane, Grace and Miriam a hug. They felt so good in his arms. His precious daughters. It was 8:00 p.m. and his plane for Chicago was leaving Nairobi in an hour. Even if he left now, he might not make it in time. The matatu that was taking him into Nairobi broke down at 4:00 that afternoon. Three hours later it still wasn't working. *God,* he prayed. *If You want me to attend the Youth For Christ conference in Chicago, I pray that this vehicle will get fixed.*

And moments later they were on their way.

"Goodbye, Dad," the girls said.

"Goodbye, my girls. I love you and I will see you as soon as I get back." He kissed each of them and turned to Esther. "I love you."

She wrapped her arms around him. They were quiet for a moment. "I love you, too," she said. "Be safe."

He nodded and left.

He was the last passenger to arrive at the gate. The flight attendant looked at the seating chart.

"The plane is full," she said, looking at his ticket. It was another issue in a whole line of problems with this trip. Even the embassy in Nairobi had initially refused his visa to the USA. Esther prayed for her husband, and the embassy changed their mind. Now here he was being told the plane was overbooked. "But," the flight attendant said, "I can give you a seat in first class."

Charles smiled. "That would be fine."

They hurried him down to the plane, where they showed him his seat. He had no baggage; he had long since given most of his clothes to the children. He carried with him only a small bag and his Bible. He sat down and the plane taxied to the runway. He glanced at his watch, thinking that in fourteen hours or so, depending on the connection, he would be seeing his good friend, Glenn Parish, again. The plane took off. *Everything is in Your hand, LORD,* he prayed. *You know that I'm suffering with typhoid—so I pray for Your healing hand upon me. Whatever You want me to do on this trip—it is in Your hand.*

And from that moment on, nothing on the trip went as planned.

When he arrived in London, the airline gave him another first-class ticket for Chicago. A friend picked him up from the airport, gave him some money and took him to the conference in Chicago. After the seven-day conference, he flew to South Carolina to meet with Glenn and Jen Parish. There he gave his testimony to ten people at a Bible study. He spoke about his passion for reaching the street children, his love for the Bible and the power of God. The people gathered in that living room listened to a man who was living everything he spoke about. They felt the sense of mission in his spirit, the calling on his life. There was something unique about Charles, something they had never encountered before. What was it about a man that would make him give up all his security, all his money, to help the street children? Why would a man put himself and his family at such great risk?

When he left, they handed him three envelopes. He hadn't spoken of finances, hadn't even mentioned his ongoing need for support. Yet they had given to him. And it encouraged him. He sat down in the car and waved goodbye to the people. As Glenn drove to Columbia Bible College, Charles realized that people give when they are touched by a ministry. And when they give, they give freely. He opened the first envelope. Sixteen-hundred dollars US. Cash. His heart nearly stopped. He opened the second envelope. Six-hundred dollars US. Cash. He closed his eyes in gratitude. How many hundreds of meals could he provide with this money? He held the third envelope in his hand. He had already received much more than he expected. He needed every penny of it. And then some. But he hadn't come with the expectation of receiving anything. Still, here it was.

With more on the way.

He tore open the next envelope. Instead of finding another wad of bills he found a small piece of paper. A cheque. He pulled it out.

Ten-thousand dollars US.

He said nothing. How could he? Ten thousand? His eyes felt the sting of tears. He closed them. He heard the singing of his orphan children thousands of miles away. The unmistakable conviction in their voices as they sang from memory. Their smiling faces flashed in his mind's eye. He felt their arms around him. He saw the hope in their eyes. The meals. The school books. The medicines. The materials for the sheet-metal dormitories. The cheque in his hand.

He spoke to students at Columbia Bible College about the power of God. When he was finished, they stood up and clapped. He spoke on campus radio. He stayed there a week, sharing about Christ and encouraging the students to listen to God's voice speaking to them in their lives.

An American lady who had been to Kenya heard his testimony and invited him to come to New Jersey. He wasn't supposed to go there. Like most of the trip, this would be another unscheduled stop. He was supposed to be in Winnipeg, Canada, next. But she insisted. There was a look of desperation in her eyes, the kind a mother has when she's tried everything and realizes she's out of hope.

"All right," Charles said. "When I'm done here, I'll come meet you at your home."

"This means so much to me," she said, convincing Charles his promise of visiting her had given her an optimism she hadn't known in quite some time.

She paid his way there. He took a plane and then got on a train. She met him at the train station. It was raining.

"Thank you for coming," she said as they got into her car.

"How is your family?" Charles asked, not out of a sense of wanting to make conversation but out of a genuine interest in her situation.

"That's why I've asked you to come," she said. "I've heard that you are a man who works miracles."

When they arrived at her home, she made him a cup of tea. Her face revealed her anxiety. It seemed to Charles that she had been spending the entire day waiting for this exact moment.

"I have a husband who works as a bank manager in New York," she began. "He'll be home soon. He's glad you're here. I'm glad you're here."

"Thank you for inviting me."

She explained that she had two sons. One was in university. Both she and her husband spoke with him often. "My other son is Andrew." She stopped for a moment and felt the burden of what she was about to say. "He's in high school. At least that's what I think." She stopped again, and it looked to Charles like she was fighting back tears. "He lives in New York." She exhaled and realized now was as good a time as any to come out with the truth. "He's in a gang, Charles. We haven't talked to him since…I don't know when. It's been a long time since we really talked. The last time I heard his voice was…" She closed her eyes and put her cup of tea down on the table.

It was the last thing on her mind right now.

"I don't know what happened. Six months ago he left to join a gang. He's turned into a…I don't even know what to call it. He terrorizes people with guns and violence. We've prayed for him. Oh, how we've prayed. But nothing has happened. I have no hope for him any more. We've done everything we can."

Charles felt her pain. He knew about bad family situations. He knew about children who ran away from home. And while she had run out of hope and felt her situation seemed impossible, he knew of dozens of situations where the worst circumstances had been overcome.

In his own life, for example.

"I know that you pray for people," she said. "That you pray for their healing. I know you have committed yourself to street children. This is why I've asked you to come. I want you to pray for my son to come back home."

In that instant, Charles felt a heartbeat away from regretting this trip to New Jersey. What if he prayed and the miracle didn't happen? Here she had gone to all the trouble to have him come to her home. What if things didn't work out? What would that do to her fragile faith?

It was a big test. A trial. He prayed with her and then went to a private room, where he got down on his knees. He began to cry. *God, You can see this woman is trusting that if I pray You are going to do something great. I pray right now in Jesus' name that You are not going to shame Your servant. Make this happen so that she will remain in Your Word.*

Later that evening they had dinner together with some friends. They had only been eating for about five minutes when the phone rang. The mother answered the phone.

"Hello?"

There was a pause on the other end of the line.

"Hello?" she said again.

"This is your son, Andrew," the voice said. "It's been a long time since I've spoken to you."

She cried as she began to talk with her son. They talked for a few minutes as she asked questions about how he was doing, whether he was getting enough to eat and if he had enough money. "I have an African friend here," she said. "Can you come over? I would love for you to meet him."

Andrew said he wasn't able to come but suggested her African friend come to see him.

They got into the car. It was seven o'clock and growing dark. She followed the directions he gave on the phone, which led them to an isolated area, far from any residential homes.

When they arrived at the address they saw an old, neglected house with one dim light on. It was pitch black outside, and Charles felt the uncertainty of being in a place that has a bad reputation.

"That's him," she said, feeling the relief a mother feels when she sees her long-lost child. "That's Andrew."

Andrew stood on the porch with his friend. He didn't wave. Didn't even acknowledge their presence. It added to Charles' nervousness. Maybe Andrew didn't believe the story his mother told him on the phone. Maybe he thought Charles was an undercover police officer acting on a tip to one of Andrew's crimes. Charles was afraid that if something went wrong here he would be leaving his wife and family in Kenya to take care of all of the orphans on their own.

"I'll go see him by myself," Charles said, stepping out of the car. Even though his mind was telling him this was suicide, his faith was telling him it was the right choice. Charles knew this wasn't about him. It wasn't his mission. He was here to help in whatever way he could. They had found Andrew through prayer, and the moment Charles' foot touched the ground his fear left him and was replaced with a confidence that God was, indeed, watching over him.

"Hi, how are you doing?" Charles said to both of them.

The mother couldn't stop herself from leaving the car. She opened the door and kept her eyes fixed on her boy. *Is he healthy? How is he doing? Is he in trouble? Is he all right?*

The boys gave a slight nod to Charles. No verbal reply.

"My name is Mulli. Charles Mulli." Charles and the mother came close enough to stand in the light. She felt a burden lifting as she saw her boy in clear view. All those anxious nights wondering if he was dead, beaten up, tripped out—all of those could be put to rest. At least for tonight.

"I was a street child myself. My parents abandoned me, and I learned to live on my own. My parents hated me."

Andrew listened, while his friend, at best, tolerated the discussion. The fear of Charles being a cop disappeared.

"I came to realize there was Someone who loved me so much. I gave my life to Christ. God changed my life and showed me a plan for my life."

Andrew's friend had had enough. He was ready to leave. God. Christ. Plan for life. No, that wasn't right. That just wasn't right. But Andrew was captivated. Simple words from a simple man, yet he felt the passion in his voice and realized that this African man had something he did not.

"Could I pray for you?" Charles asked, expecting a yes.

"No," the friend replied in a cool, even tone of voice, as though he had just been waiting for the moment to reject him. He motioned to Andrew that they should go back inside.

"I'd like you to pray for me," Andrew said. His friend stood there, shocked.

Charles closed his eyes. Andrew and his mother did as well. The friend did not. He would have no part in this stupidity.

"God, you have created this moment. You have brought us together. May you bless these two boys."

When he finished praying, Andrew stepped into the light and hugged his mother. She cried, feeling the connection that comes with physical touch.

"I'll be coming home tomorrow, Mom," he said.

"Okay," his mother whispered in-between tears.

"Is that all right?"

"That's all right."

"Even after all this time?"

"Even after all this time."

He hugged Charles as well. They said goodbye. The friend went in first. Andrew waited until his mother and Charles got into the car and drove off.

Healings. Demonic deliverance. Charles had seen countless miracles. But as he sat in that car feeling the parents' joy over their son who was coming home, it occurred to him that the restoration of relationships was truly the greatest miracle of all. From the mother's plea in South Carolina only a day earlier to a re-established relationship in

New York the next, Charles admired God once again for what He had accomplished. *Thank You, God.*

Andrew did come home the next day. And while he struggled against the pull of his former friends who wanted him to come back to the streets, he instead returned to school, where he was eventually elected president. He later joined Mully Children's Family in Africa for a month to see his "father" who had saved him from the path down which he was heading. He went on to study and found work as a social worker, helping children with troubled lives.

The next day Charles got on a plane to Canada. From there he flew to Germany and stayed at the home of Mr. and Mrs. Schaeffer in the city of Gomaringen. While having lunch with them, they heard pounding at the door, a desperate pounding that tells you something is very, very wrong.

Mrs. Schaeffer went to the door. She opened it and immediately wished she hadn't. A woman stood there, shouting and screaming about things that didn't make sense. Her eyes had a hint of craziness in them. She barged her way into the house. Her voice echoed off the walls, bringing panic into what had been a calm lunch. The Schaeffers knew her. She was a friend of the family who suffered from mental illness.

When they were able to settle her down, she told them she was to be admitted to the psychiatric ward. Her condition was getting worse. She had managed to leave the grounds for fear they would keep her there. She felt the uncertainty of a future in a lock-down ward and had lost what little grip of reality she had left.

Her hands trembled. Her eyes darted left and right as if looking for those men in white coats who were about to barge in at any moment and take her away. They wouldn't be able to find her. Not here. Not now. But what if they did? Would they be tougher on her? Would they put her in a cell?

Charles and the Schaeffers laid hands on her head.

"God, You see this woman who is suffering terribly," Charles prayed. "I ask in Jesus' name that You will touch her, that You will change and heal her."

In that moment the panic left her. The atmosphere in the room changed from fear and uncertainty to peace and reassurance. That suspicious look left her eyes. She breathed like a normal person. They felt the strange shift in attitude, wondering how it could possibly have changed this fast.

They took her to the psychiatric hospital. The doctors recognized her. After numerous tests she was released, without ever having to spend another night on the hospital property, provided she stayed on a few minor prescribed medications.

Charles went on to preach at numerous schools and churches in Germany. At one school, the children ran out after he had finished speaking, shouting "Mulli! Mulli!" Police officers saw it and stopped Charles, much the way many of the police officers in Eldoret did when they questioned him about his work with the street children and why he was helping those who were accused of robbery. Charles explained he was there to preach about Jesus Christ. But the German police officers weren't interested. They arrested him and took him to the police station. But after further questioning they found no reason to lay charges, so they released him.

People throughout North America and Europe had welcomed Charles on his trip. Many had donated funds without him even asking. He later used the money to buy food and pay for renovations to the house, which became increasingly necessary because the children who were raised on the streets didn't take care of things very well.

He got back on the plane to London and remembered all the people he had seen on his trip to the West. In the years that followed, people in North America, Europe, Australia and Israel joined his much-needed financial and prayer support team to partner with him in the ministry to which he had dedicated his life.

CHAPTER 25

Charles read the story in the *Standard Paper*. He'd been interviewed by a reporter on his work with the street children. But as he read the article, he realized that while he had a clear vision of his life's mission, there were others who had a harder time seeing it through his eyes.

> *"Mr. Mulli, you threw all the wealth to the dogs. Why did you think of giving to the street children who will never help you and will never reform?"*

He put the paper down on the table. *Dogs? I threw my wealth to the dogs? I don't think so*. It bothered him that people could refer to street children that way. Where was the inherent value of human life? Where was the compassion? What gave a reporter the right to look down on children who didn't have the advantages he had? And the part about the children never helping him. Was that the purpose of life? To only help those who could help you in return? The reporter was also dead wrong about children never reforming. Most—not all—of the children Charles had rescued from the streets were changing. Right before his very eyes. They were in school. His school. Following the Kenyan curriculum. They were learning about Christ. Every day they had a devotional time when they sang about Jesus and heard a word of encouragement from either Charles, Esther or one of their children. They knew about love. Real love. The kind of love that is willing to leave lofty places to go into the streets to meet them where they were. God *was* reforming them.

The reporters and the church people who scoffed at him had no idea what they were talking about.

Yet because of his ministry with the children and his gift for evangelism, Charles continued to be called to preach in various schools and churches.

In 1993, he invited a team of six young people from different churches to join him in going to Baringo (about 150 kilometres from Eldoret) in the Rift Valley for an evening of preaching, drama and singing. A school of 1,200 boys and girls invited him to give a weekend challenge to encourage them in the faith.

They arrived at 4:00 p.m., and Charles asked the person in charge if his team could go to Lake Bogoria, about 15 kilometres from the school, to have a prayer time along the seashore. They arrived at the waterfront and prayed for God to do something powerful among the children. He prayed for the anointing to preach and to be prepared spiritually by the LORD for what they were about to do. They sang songs under the trees while being swarmed by a variety of bugs known only to Africa. Pink flamingos passed by near the water. While they sang, Charles felt the power of the Holy Spirit on his life.

Behind them, up on the highway, they heard a number of cars slowing down. Charles turned and saw a motorcade approaching. A distinguished man stepped out. Charles recognized him.

It was Kenyan president Daniel Moi.

He came down to the lake to stand near the flamingos. He walked along the beach and, hearing the group's singing, he came closer. They stopped singing.

"Hello," Moi said.

Charles greeted him. Moi remembered Charles. Even after all this time, he remembered the man he once met at the pastors' conference and at the church in Eldoret. Charles explained why they were here.

"I am so glad that someone like you has come with these young people to pray and to intercede for students. It is something we need in this country."

They talked a while longer, and just as Moi was about to leave, he said, "I want to bless you with a small gift. Would you come to the car with me?"

Charles followed him up to the motorcade. The driver opened the door for Moi, who sat down in the back seat and emerged a few moments later. In his hand he held an envelope, which he gave to Charles.

"I want you to have this," he said.

Charles felt the weight of the envelope. It made him wonder how much was inside.

"Here are 20,000 shillings," Moi said. "It's not much, but it's what I have to offer you."

"It is a lot," Charles replied. "This will feed all the orphans for over a month."

Moi laughed. "Then I'm glad it will be put to good use."

Moi got back in his car and left. Charles returned to the team and told them what had just happened. It was the first time an African had contributed to his ministry.

At 6:30 they left the bugs and flamingos and went back to the school. They felt energized. The confidence of the presence of Christ burned within them. Their time of prayer and singing had prepared them spiritually to start the meeting. This was important. Because they were going to need it for what they were about to encounter.

They were waiting for them. A boy, a girl and a female teacher. They stood outside the packed auditorium, looking for the man they hoped would finally be the solution to their problems. Charles and the team entered the school.

"Mr. Mulli!" the teacher shouted, hurrying towards them. "Mr. Mulli!"

Charles turned around to see the teacher holding the girl and boy by their hands as they headed towards him. She stopped in front of him.

"Please help them," she said, out of breath. Her face was filled with anxiety. She spoke at a rapid pace, as though already trying to counter any reasons he might have for not wanting to help them.

"What is it?"

"These children. They are in need of your help. God's help. I've heard what you've done. We all have. We know that God works through you to help people who are being..." She stopped speaking as if mentioning the problem might somehow make it worse. She fixed her eyes on his and spoke in a quiet voice so as not to disturb the children. "We think..." She couldn't get the words out. She looked to the left and to the right as though some creature had been stalking her and was ready to pounce on her at the mention of the problem. She swallowed. They needed help. Desperately. And besides, this wasn't just affecting the boy and girl. It was affecting her. It was affecting all of them. She took in a breath. "I think they're possessed," she said.

She clenched her teeth as if forcing herself not to say anything more.

Charles said nothing. He only nodded and then got down on his knees to be at the children's level. They stepped closer to him. Everything except their eyes looked normal. There was a lifeless dullness to their eyes. No shine. No energy. No excitement.

"How are you?" Charles asked in a soft voice.

The children didn't respond.

"How are you feeling?" Charles asked, hoping to draw one of them into conversation.

"I'm scared," the girl whispered.

And the moment she said that, the hallway seemed to darken. Everything became quiet. It was as though they were the only people in the entire school.

"What are you scared about?" Charles asked.

She looked at the boy beside her, wondering if it was all right to be talking about their problem with a stranger. The boy gave no reply, so she continued.

"I see images," she said. She couldn't have been more than ten. Small build. Soft, nervous voice.

"What kind of images?" Charles asked.

She closed her eyes and pressed her lips together. The teacher got down on her knees and put her arms around her. "It's happening again. Please. Please, you have to do something."

"Are you seeing those images now?" Charles asked.

She nodded and then began to shake her head back and forth, trying to get rid of whatever was being pumped into her young mind.

Charles laid his hand on top of her head, feeling her body twitch as he sensed the horror of those images. "Father, in the name of Jesus Christ, You see how this girl is suffering. By the name of Your Son Jesus Christ, I command these spirits who are attacking her to be gone."

She stopped shaking. She kept her eyes shut and her face tensed, as if waiting for another onslaught. But it never came. She waited, feeling for the first time what it was like to be free from those haunting pictures in her mind.

She opened her eyes and saw Charles.

"How do you feel?" he asked.

She blinked her eyes. They were gone. They were really gone. She wasn't even able to remember what it felt like to be under that curse. A faint glimmer of hope burned in her eyes. A moment without fear. A moment without the images.

"They're gone. They're really gone." She looked up at Charles. "Are they coming back?"

"No. They are not coming back. Do you have a Bible?"

"Yes."

"Are you reading it?"

"I am."

"That is good."

"How do you know they are not coming back?"

"Because Jesus has taken them away and because you have decided to follow Him."

She nodded her head. Charles turned to the boy.

"Hello," Charles said.

The boy's eyes shot back and forth, as if some unseen power inside him was trying to avoid looking at Charles.

"My name is Charles Mulli, and I love you very much."

The boy's teeth began to chatter. It felt cold. He breathed in short slow bursts, becoming aware that something bad was about to happen.

"Are you all right?" Charles asked.

The boy looked behind him. There was nothing there. He glanced back again. Still nothing.

"I see it," he said.

Charles looked behind the boy and saw the empty hallway.

"See what?" Charles asked.

"I do. I see it."

"There's nothing there. There's nothing behind you."

"Yes, there is. It's everywhere. I see it everywhere I go."

"What do you see?"

The boy swallowed. His breathing became louder. His eyes refused to remain still as they scanned around Charles.

"I've seen it for over two years. It comes, and I can't do anything to stop it."

"What comes? You can tell me. What comes?"

A pulse shot through the boy. It looked like an electric current zipped through him. It was inhuman. Panic set in the boy's eyes.

"It comes out of nowhere. It wants to kill me. It comes out of the shadows. When I'm in bed. When I walk down the hallway at school. When I'm in the fields. It comes especially at night. It must know. It comes to kill me." He closed his eyes, trying to get the picture of the beast out of his mind. But retreating to that world only made things more difficult. He opened his eyes.

"It will kill me."

"No, it will not."

"Yes. Eventually it will. I can not escape from it forever."

"I know a Power greater than what you see."

"Not even the hospital can help me."

"I know Someone who can help."

"It is too powerful. It knows me. It knows my thoughts. It's only a matter of time now."

"Jesus Christ can set you free."

The boy suddenly slammed down to the ground. It was as if some invisible man had smashed into him to make him fall like that. His body twisted and contorted, writhing in agony.

The teacher screamed. She had seen this dozens of times before, yet each time it happened she felt the same fear. She stepped back, trying not to contract whatever spirit was attacking this child.

The boy shouted and screamed in a revolting, throaty language that Charles did not understand.

He reached his hand down to the boy and laid it on his head.

"Father," he said. "You are in control. You are more powerful than what is in this boy's mind. Your blood has destroyed Satan. Your blood has destroyed evil. In the name of Jesus Christ, I command this demon to go."

The boy let out a sickening scream. It hurt their ears to hear it.

And then everything went quiet.

The calm after the storm.

The boy began to cry. Charles picked him up from the ground and got him back on his feet. The teacher watched in amazement, trying to understand how an impossible problem of over two years could vanish in an instant.

The boy looked at Charles with steady eyes. No dashing around. No panic. Just bright brown eyes looking up at Charles as the boy felt the relief of being set free.

"It's gone," the boy whispered.

"And it's not coming back," Charles replied. He reached for the girl's hand. She gave him her hand and came closer. "Both of you have experienced a miracle."

"How did you do that?" she asked.

"I didn't do anything," he said. "It was Jesus Christ who did it. It is the power of Jesus who died on the cross for you that destroyed those images in your minds. He made both of you, and He wants to live His life in you."

"Jesus did that?"

"Yes."

"Because He loves us?" the boy asked.

"That's right."

"Why does He love us?" the girl asked.

"Because that's what God does."

After the singing and drama, Charles stood up and addressed the massive auditorium, telling them about the love and power of God. He invited those children who wanted to surrender their lives to Jesus Christ to come to the front and pray for God to forgive their sins and make them His children. One-hundred-eighty-five children gave their lives to Christ that night.

Including the boy and girl.

CHAPTER 26

By 1994, the home in Eldoret had become too crowded. The Mullis were caring for about 200 children, and it placed an impossible demand on the property. They had built metal-siding dormitories and makeshift classrooms, which the children had long since outgrown. They needed more money, and they needed more space. Charles and Esther had sold off all of their businesses and all of their properties—save two. All they had left was the home in Eldoret and their retirement property in Ndalani.

It was situated on the long and winding Thika River. Unspoiled. Uninhabited. Undeveloped. But to the imaginative eyes of Charles Mulli it showed unbelievable potential. He had the property all mapped out. He wanted to build a large home for his family within a stone's throw of the river. They would plant fruit trees, too—mangos, lemons, bananas. Their retirement home. Their future.

It was the very last of what they could call their own.

"It's all we have left," Esther said as she and Charles cleaned up. They had organized a festival day for the children, and now that most of them were in bed, they had time to get things ready for tomorrow.

"I know," Charles said. "I love that place."

"It will never be ours again. Just like this home will never be ours."

"Does that bother you?"

"The Ndalani property or this one?"

"Both."

Esther took a rag and cleaned off one of the tables. "I love these children, Charles."

"I know you do. That's evident in everything you do, Esther."

"At first I thought you were crazy." They laughed. His laugh was louder than hers, filling the entire property behind the house, which was comprised of the dormitories and the school. "The kids. Stealing things from our home. Breaking things. Some of them running away and going right back into prostitution and the gangs from which you saved them. You go out looking for them again and bring them back to our home. Sometimes I thought, what is the matter with these kids?"

Charles laughed again. He had rescued a number of street children from their brutal lives. And yet, some had retained the strange disposition to leave the path of hope and return to destruction.

"And now they have not just become part of our lives. They *are* our lives. I'm not trying to make it sound like they are a higher priority than Christ…"

"I understand," Charles said.

"It makes me wonder, Charles. It makes me wonder what will become of us. It's too big for us to handle on our own, and I wonder what kind of future we are building for our own children. And I wonder where we will go when it finally becomes too much. If we give the property away, we have no security. We have no recourse. We once had the businesses, the properties, the friends. Now we will have nothing." She caught herself again. "Nothing but God, of course, but you know what I mean."

"I do."

"And you still want to sell it?"

"You don't?"

"I'm asking you," Esther said.

"I wonder how we can keep that property while we have no place to expand the school."

"Then the decision is made."

"Is it your decision?" Charles looked at her to ensure they were together in this. "Is it your decision, too?"

Esther put the rag back into the pail of water. "Yes, Charles," she said with a look that was both relieved the decision was made and also anxious about what it meant to have no further recourse.

They held the dedication services for MCF Ndalani on August 20, 1994. About 400 people from Nairobi and Ndalani gathered under a golden and merciless sun to pray over the dedication of the property.

After Charles spoke the final prayer, people stayed to eat and meet with one another. Their eight biological children—Jane, Grace, Miriam, Ndondo, Kaleli, Mueni, Isaac and Dickson—were in charge of the food. They served the people with undivided attention. All except Jane, who had other things on her mind.

She was getting married the following day.

The entire 200-member MCF choir packed out the stage to sing for Jane at her wedding in Nairobi. The church loved it. Street kids who had been given a new beginning were singing for Jane at her new beginning.

Charles sent two workers to Ndalani to settle the property by starting farms. They got the barren land ready for the arrival of seventeen boys from the Eldoret site in 1995. They were troublemakers, and Charles thought the best thing for them was to get them out onto the land, where they could see life from a different perspective. Together with two teachers, the group pioneered the MCF Ndalani settlement. They had a program of schooling, farming and carpentry that integrated the educational, spiritual, physical and work aspects of their lives. The boys turned their lives around and thrived in their new environment.

In addition to being a father to some two hundred children, running a ministry and evangelizing at crusades where hundreds were getting saved, Charles decided to enrol at the Missionary College in Eldoret. He studied under Pastor Kitonyi, a man with a deep, honest laugh that was equally matched by his conviction and passion for reaching the street children of Eldoret and beyond.

Charles went to school during the week and on weekends visited the boys in Ndalani. He got to know them by talking with them under the stars and sometimes on the banks of the Thika River among the incredible trees. There, the boys opened up about their drug addicted mothers who made *changa'a* to support themselves but could not earn enough for the boys, forcing them on to the streets.

They told Charles what they had become. Some of them were harmless street boys who went begging from place to place, sleeping under store roofs. But others had tougher stories. Gang stories. Violent stories. Troubled pasts. For the first time some of them discussed how they had raped girls. This didn't surprise Charles. Many of the girls he rescued had been raped. While the streets were tough places for boys, they were horrendous for girls.

Charles was the only person on earth who had ever taken the time to listen to the boys and offer them the love they needed to know that in spite of everything they were, in spite of everything they had done, and in spite of everything that had been done to them, they were still precious to God.

On December 31, 1995, Charles arranged the mass migration of all the boys in grades two to seven (some 220 in all) to Ndalani, along with the required teachers and workers. Some of the children refused. They stayed in Eldoret. But most moved to their new home, some 460 kilometres south to an area none of them had ever heard of.

They lived in dorms made of corrugated metal. Most of them slept two to a bed. Some were fortunate enough to have mattresses. Those that didn't had to sleep on slats. They drew their drinking water from the Thika River, which had been serving the boys well for months, but the new children were not used to it. The river carried numerous waterborne diseases that made twenty to thirty children sick each week until all of them became accustomed to it. They assumed their water problem was solved.

But they would soon be proven wrong.

The children combined their schoolwork with working on the farms or doing chores. They turned the property into a beautiful environment. Each child was involved in a Bible study group. Most of them were eager to join choirs that performed at daily devotional times for the whole school. And they always found time to swim each day after their lunch break to cool down from the unrelenting heat. The children had to adjust to the change in elevation. Eldoret was at an elevation of 2,200 metres while Ndalani was at 975 metres. The lower elevation meant higher temperatures, with 40 degrees Celsius (104F) not being uncommon.

But while the children fell in love with their new way of life, the villagers in the area had become increasingly upset that these former prostitutes and thugs had infiltrated their ranks.

The actual site was located in the country, ten kilometres from the town of Ndalani, so the children weren't as near other homes as they were in Eldoret. But sometimes presence is enough to destroy peace, and the villagers wanted them out.

Located in the Kamba tribe region, Ndalani was not made up of villagers who were interested in accepting any of the other tribes. Each of the forty-two tribes in Kenya had their geographical area, their settlement, their problems. Why couldn't Charles, a Kamba man himself, understand that? Why did he bring this mix of Kikuyu, Luo, Luhya, Kamba and Masai children and cause unrest among the people? There was no reason for it. The children were a threat in Eldoret. They were a threat in Ndalani.

The Ndalani elders summoned Charles to a meeting in the town centre with the chief. Charles came in and sat down at a small table opposite a group of men. A man near the entrance closed the door. It was cool inside that small room. Even though it was broad daylight, there were few windows, making it feel later than it was.

"Why did you choose to bring these kids—these criminals—to us?"

Charles recognized the man as a ruling official who was still there from the time they had almost caned his father to death. In that instant he saw his father lying face down on the ground. He heard that first stick come crashing down on his back. He saw the horrifying expression on Daudi's face as he cringed in pain and then looked with desperation at Charles, hoping against all odds that his son would rescue him from the punishment he deserved.

"We expected someone like you to bring development. To improve our land. You are Kamba, and you are successful. You are our son. Look at you. You have acquired wealth. You can help this community. But what do you do instead? You come with thugs. Why do you do this? Why can't you come alone?"

Charles closed his eyes a moment, as if doing so could remove the images of his father from his mind.

"You are partly correct. You see, these children were thugs. They aren't any more. They have changed."

"How can you be sure?" another official asked. "The town hates you. They want to run you and your children out. And if they decide to do that, there is no stopping them!"

"They won't."

"They will, Charles."

"Nobody is sending us anywhere."

"Charles, you have to understand how angry people are. There's no reasoning with them. You've brought different tribes to our land. That infuriates people. And not only that, you have caused widespread panic in Ndalani because you have brought prostitutes and gang members here."

"I'm telling you, they aren't going to be a problem."

"Can you guarantee the town's security?"

"I can guarantee the town's security."

Charles said that as an instinctive response. But after he had a chance to think about his answer, it occurred to him that, at best, he could only *hope* that nothing would go wrong. Besides, he had to say it. If he didn't, the village would have gone into a frenzy—as they were prone to doing. Like at canings, for instance.

"You can?"

There was no turning back. Charles trusted that God would change the lives of the children and that they would not be a problem in the village.

"I can."

"Very well," the official said. "Then my best wishes to you, Charles. To you and your whole group. You'll need it. Raising that many street children with so few resources is madness."

CHAPTER 27

Even though the people of Ndalani decided to accept the children, or at least not run them out of town, the local educational authorities had not been won over. The issue of tribalism prevented them from granting Charles a school exam licence for these children, who were a mixture of mostly non-Kamba tribes. Ndalani was in the Yatta division of the Machakos district. There were 940 schools in that district, and all of them were Kamba. The officials responsible for the eleven schools in the Ndalani area did not want to accept Charles' application, because they feared that by including these street children from Eldoret, the Ndalani overall grade average would go down.

"We know the street children will never accomplish anything," they told him. "We are not granting you any authority to start a school."

So Charles went to the Machakos district to have the Ndalani officials' decision overturned. But the Machakos district refused him as well. So Charles inquired about making an appointment with the minister of education, who would be the final authority on whether abandoned children deserved the right to be educated. MCF teachers and students prayed for God to intervene so that the minister might have compassion and see the value of education for them.

Two months later Charles received permission to come for a meeting. That in itself was cutting it close. The date for the meeting was only three days before the cut-off point for granting licences for that year. Kenya requires all children wishing to continue on in their studies to pass national practice exams after standard eight (grade eight) to allow them into secondary school, and also after form four (grade twelve) to allow the top percent into university. MCF had children in the grade eight category and had already prepared them for their KCPE (Kenya Certificate of Primary Education).

Charles made the trip to Nairobi and met with the minister of education. He was not from the Kamba tribe, which, in and of itself, encouraged hope that perhaps he would see outside of the box of tribalism.

"What?" the minister shouted. He had come across as a gentle, calm sort of fellow, yet when they met in his office and Charles told him the situation, the minister lost his cool. "They are rejecting you?"

"That's correct."

"Why?"

That put Charles in a bit of a bind. If he told the minister the real reason why the local and district level authorities had turned him down, he would be causing problems for them. Then again, exposing them for what they were might be a good thing.

"You have to ask them," Charles said.

So the minister did. He got on the phone and called the Machakos district. He berated them for their foolishness and then wrote a letter overruling their decision and ordering them to grant MCF the right to take the exams.

As Charles walked out of the office, he said a prayer of thanks to God and felt the pride of being able to grant his children the opportunity to take grade eight exams.

Something he himself was never able to do.

In November of 1996, Mully Children's Family took their first standardized exams. The entire family gathered together for a special prayer of dedication for the students. They asked God to give them victory in their hands. And then, the children went to their week-long exams to prove their mettle to the local and district authorities.

Months later the minister of education's office gave the results of all of Kenya's exams to the districts to hand back to their schools. Otieno from MCF drove to get the results and brought them back. Charles and Jacob opened the results together. And what they saw shocked them.

MCF got the highest marks among the eleven Ndalani schools. Not only that, but they were highest among the 124 schools in the Yatta division. And then they discovered that of the 940 schools in the Machakos district, they were the best.

MCF had raised the average in every zone.

Out of the thousands of schools across Kenya, MCF placed in the top 100. The educational authorities in the Machakos district couldn't believe it. The children they had neglected, the ones they thought were nothing, had brought them victory.

That evening MCF had a celebration service. Under the African sky the children clapped and sang with such conviction that they could be heard all the way up to the main road. The children who wrote the exams felt honoured in succeeding at something in which they weren't meant to do well. They were the best. They had succeeded.

God had given them victory.

MCF continued to do well in education, to such a degree that the local people of the Ndalani, who had once wanted them out, were now begging for a chance to have their own children attend the school. Charles told them MCF could only help orphans, and so he took in sixty children from the Ndalani area who were without parents. Together they took the lowest of the low, and by God's guidance they were transformed into a tour de force, both in education and in sports.

MCF became well known for their running, football and karate programs. Surrounding schools wondered why MCF was taking all the trophies in both the area and divisional school competitions. They had even won a science competition at the Yatta divisional level for the development of new technologies. They won it by developing a new animal feed ration, made by using an innovative and cheaper method of combining all the necessary components of protein, carbohydrates, fat and vitamins.

They made a road trip in 1997 to play in the playoffs for the Yatta divisional championships in football. Among the 124 schools, they made it to the finals and won. When the referee blew the final whistle, the MCF team shouted, the way winning teams do, as they rushed together to congratulate each other. The teachers who had made the trip ran onto the field as well. Here they were. Kids from all over. Kids with terrible backgrounds. Kids from different tribes. All of them had been rescued and had managed to rise above it and feel the camaraderie of victory.

The sixty or so MCF boys got back on the large trailer pulled by a tractor and started the long trek back to Ndalani. They passed their trophies around for each of them to admire and sang praise and worship songs as they bumped along the road. Suddenly the tractor came to a stop. The boys looked out ahead. Large rocks had been placed in the road.

Just then, over 200 boys from two of the surrounding schools charged the trailer, throwing rocks and cursing at them. They swore at the top of their lungs that they were going to steal the trophies and kill them by beating them senseless.

But the MCF boys, raised on the streets and educated in karate, were equal to the task. They jumped out of the trailer and rushed out to meet their attackers.

What followed next was a scene from a martial arts movie. Using a combination of flying kicks and closed-fisted strikes, the MCF team defended themselves. Fierce shouting and screaming erupted from the once peaceful road setting. The fighting got so intense that the MCF teachers ran away in the hopes of not being killed.

One of the MCF boys took on three assailants, each of whom held rocks in their hands ready to bash in his head. He struck the first one in the chest with a decisive sidekick, driving his heel into his attacker's sternum. It knocked the wind out of him and forced him down to the ground. The next victim made the mistake of swinging a wide punch in an attempt to strike the MCF boy on the side of the head. But the MCF boy raised his arm in a sweeping motion to block the punch. He then grabbed his opponent's wrist and pulled him closer. The MCF boy brought his right hand to his ear and smashed it down on the boy's face. They all heard a cracking sound as the boy fell to the ground screaming.

It should have been clear to the third boy that perhaps he was outclassed. But like most people when they are overcome with anger, the boy was not rational and would not be outdone by these pathetic, useless street kids who didn't deserve to be here. They locked on to each other's eyes, both waiting to see who would attack first.

The MCF boy switched his stance so that his right leg was back and his left leg forward. The attacker charged him. In a calm, cool and almost rehearsed movement, the MCF boy twisted his hips, turned to face the other direction and looked over his shoulder as he extended his right leg back to thrust his heel into the assailant's hips. He made perfect contact. There was a disgusting crack. His opponent dropped to the ground. He screamed with such intensity that it caused other attackers fighting nearby to stop fighting. The MCF boy charged after more of the assailants to give assistance to his other MCF friends. Within minutes, dozens of the attackers lay on the ground bleeding from their noses and mouths. Some of them had broken bones. Some were in that precarious place between consciousness and unconsciousness.

The police arrived and dispersed the remaining attackers, who were more than happy to leave without suffering the same fate as their comrades who would no doubt be taking weeks, if not months, to mend. The police arrested some of the attackers and helped clear the road for the MCF students to continue on their way home.

They got back on their trailer and rode off into the sunset singing their songs.

Not one of them had been hurt.

CHAPTER 28

Charles was in Eldoret when he received the news about the fight. As he listened to Otieno on the other end of the phone telling him about it, he felt sad to hear what had happened. He put down the phone and left Eldoret for Ndalani to talk with his boys.

On the six-hour drive down, he wondered about what to say. Could he blame them for what happened? The karate instruction was meant to give children a means of staying physically fit. But wasn't it also there for practical purposes like this? Should they have stayed in the trailer and been beaten, or were they right in defending themselves?

He wanted to talk with the boys about the tension between peaceful resolution and the need, or the right, for defence. They'd hurt some of their attackers, resulting in a broken rib and a few broken bones. But this was nothing for the MCF boys. How could it compare?

On the streets they had killed people.

Charles met with them in one of the classrooms. They sat down in used wooden desks. He stood at the front and looked out at his championship football team. It felt so good to see them. Their faces were full of accomplishment and dignity. They weren't street kids. They were his kids. His boys.

"Thank you for coming to meet with me."

They gave no response. They waited. Some of those new to the school expected what they had received on the street—harsh treatment from anyone who didn't approve of them. Instead, they received something else.

"I am so proud of you for winning the football tournament. Out of all the 124 schools, you won. You were the best, and you proved it. I love you boys very, very much. I am so proud to call you my sons. You are not orphans. Not any more. You are my children, and you are loved because of that. You have succeeded, but even if you hadn't, I would love you all the same. My love for you is guaranteed because of who you are, not because of what you do, or do not, accomplish."

Charles cleared his voice. The boys looked at him with more purpose. They all knew why they were here.

"I understand there was an incident involving some of the students from other schools today. And I want to talk with you about karate. I think you know that here at MCF we believe that it is not good to fight. But I also know the 200 students who attacked you would have killed you had you not defended yourselves.

"I am proud of you that you are not the kind of boys who go looking for fights, that you do not want to cause harm. It is not good to fight. And we do not respond right away with fighting. We need to love people, and the best thing is to forgive the people who wrong you."

Charles stopped. He tried to sort out his message in his mind.

"In life we will always be able to respond by attacking people, whether with our hands and feet, with our words or with our actions. That option is always open to us. But this is not the way of the gospel. We are charged to love one another as Christ loves us. Does that mean we are never to defend ourselves? Does that mean we stand and get taken advantage of, even killed, for what we believe? Even Jesus Himself was killed for what He believed.

"You will always have a choice. I know many of you come from trauma on the streets. And I want you to know that fighting is the last response. I think you know that. It is often easier to fight than it is to find a way of reconciliation. The children who attacked you did the wrong thing. We all know they envied you for your success."

"Was it right or wrong?" asked the boy who had broken another boy's hip.

It was a good question. It was *the* question that all of them were wondering about. Including Charles.

"The boys should not have attacked. But they did. And in that short time there was no chance for a peaceful response. We are to love our neighbours and not quickly resort to aggression as a means of solving problems. We need to forgive. We need to be slow to anger." He paused.

"The best response, the hardest response, is to find a way of loving our neighbour, especially when it is difficult."

Charles nodded that he was finished saying what he had come to share. "Once again," he said with a smile. "I am so proud of you all. You are the best football players!"

The boys shouted and banged their fists on the desks.

"Now let's go have something to eat," Charles said. He opened the door and shook the hands of his all-star team as they left the room.

By 1997, they needed to start their own secondary school. It would be too expensive to send their students in grades nine to twelve to another institution. The decision to expand brought with it many questions. How do you start a high school? Where do we put the students? How do we enlarge the budget that is already stretched? Where do we find the teachers?

Charles took time to find a quiet place near the river late in the evening to pray about the decision. No money. No teachers. No resources.

No problem for God.

Charles was more than ready to go ahead, provided he had the assurance that this is where God wanted him.

"My King, my LORD. We need a high school. You see the need. We need teachers. We need the money. And we need buildings. The makeshift metal buildings are too hot. You can see the children in the classrooms. It is so hard for them to learn in that heat."

Charles stood up and walked along the river bank, hearing the water rush past one of the docks the children had built for swimming.

"Father, You said in Exodus that where we put our feet down and claim it, it will be given unto us."

The moment he spoke that verse, he gained confidence. He began to cry, a time-tested sign that told him he was in deep prayer with God. When he finished praying, he knew that God would answer and he knew that somehow God would provide.

Because the school had done so well in their grade eight exams, they attracted teachers, some of whom were qualified to teach at the high school level. He assigned two of them to develop the high school curriculum. Shortly thereafter, three more teachers came, expressing their interest in helping the secondary program get off the ground.

They used the carpentry, metal working and welding training the boys had been learning and coordinated their efforts to put together a construction plan for the new school. They began working on the windows, doors and gates and put a schedule together for the required materials, such as stone for the walls, concrete for the floor, wood for the roof trusses and the shingles.

The only missing ingredient was the money.

As usual, Charles did not ask people for money in his letters. He chose instead to focus on God's word and to do what He appointed him to do. It was going to work out. Somehow it would. Even before any money had come in, he gathered all the children together. Over 300 children packed onto the rickety wooden benches to hear what the man they called *Daddy* had to say.

"I am here today to tell you that soon God is going to provide for us! Look around you," Charles said. "Does anyone see a high school here?"

Some of them shook their heads.

"I'm sorry," Charles said with a laugh. "I couldn't hear you. Does anyone see a high school here?"

A number of them shouted out, "No!"

"Oh, I think there are more students here than just these few. Does anyone see a high school?"

The children shouted out, "No!"

"But guess what? There will be. There will be a school. God is going to provide a school for you. He is already bringing the teachers. He is already gathering the workers. And He is going to provide a school for you!"

The children shouted. Three hundred children cheering for God sounded like 30,000 people cheering for their favourite sports team.

"He got you off the street. He brought you here to MCF. He gave you a bed and food and clothes and a school. And now, when you finish standard eight, God is going to give you a high school!"

They clapped and shouted. Then they sang praise songs together in celebration of what God was about to do.

When the service ended, the children went off to do their chores or their homework. One of the short-term missionaries that had come to volunteer at MCF for a month sat at the back and waited until Charles had finished speaking with the teachers. When he was alone, she walked up to him.

"Mr. Mulli?" she asked.

"Yes, hello, how are you?" he asked, calling her by name. It amazed her that he remembered it. Over 300 children, thirty teachers, dozens of workers. He knew all their names, including hers.

"Mr. Mulli, how do you know that God is going to come through for you? How do you know the money is going to come through for the school?"

Charles smiled. "That is a very good question."

They sat down on a bench. Nearby, a child washed her hands under the tap and then hurried off to a late-night choir practice. In the kitchen, at the back of the open assembly area, some of the workers prepared a few items for breakfast the next morning.

"I know that you need God to provide the money," she said. "And I want it to come through, just like everyone else. But listening to you talk up there, I just see that you know He's going to do that for you. I don't have that in my life. I love God. But I just don't have the confidence that He'll do the things I ask."

Charles nodded his head as he listened. His smile had faded. The expression on his face changed to that of recognizing the struggle this young woman was having.

"Of course, I can't always say for sure what God is going to do. But there are three things that I follow when I'm praying. First, I'm not doing my own thing. I'm doing a ministry. This is 100 percent for God. So why shouldn't He want it to work out? Second, God has entrusted me to care for these children. And you can see, there are many, many children here. Not only in Ndalani but also in Eldoret. God sees this is much too much for one person. It is impossible for me to do it on my own. So He is actually responsible for these children. I am here to be His representative. And third, whatever results come is not for me but for MCF. The children were lost and had no hope. But these miracles, these provisions, they happen so the children may see and believe. And I know that God honours that. When I pray, I know in my spirit that God will act. And when I know that, there is no turning back."

She was quiet for a moment, trying to understand what he said, feeling the weight of being in the presence of someone who had a closer walk with Christ than she did.

"I wish I had your faith," she said. "I've been believing God for areas in my life that haven't worked. I sometimes wonder if I'm praying for the wrong things."

"The prayers we make individually for our own lives and families are fine. We need to pray for the benefit of ourselves and others. God answers and honours those prayers. God will bless and give to those who need the help, so don't be discouraged. God does according to His will. And we can't force God to answer our prayers."

"It's just that when I see you up there, I see something I don't have. I admire you, Mr. Mulli. I've never met anyone like you."

"And I have never met anyone like you," he said in a way that reached right inside of her. She smiled, not understanding how a man like Charles could see that in her.

"It's amazing to be here," she said. "This place. This place is going to be impossible to describe to people. I have no idea what I'm going to tell them when I go home."

"Tell them we love them," Charles said.

"I will. Thank you," she said as she stood up.

"Good night," he said, "and have a good sleep."

"You too, Mr. Mulli." She gave him a hug and walked away to prepare for her next class.

Mr. Mulli called out her name.

She turned around. "Yes?"

"One more thing."

"What's that?"

He looked at her with genuine eyes, the kind that transmit exactly what is going on inside. "Your faith is stronger than you think."

"Thank you," she said and walked off under the flying bugs to her room.

The secondary school started that same year. By 1999, all the money had arrived and brand new primary and secondary school buildings were completed.

CHAPTER 29

The first signs of trouble came when the children weren't recovering as fast as when they had first arrived. All the children got sick from the water. It was like an unofficial initiation into MCF Ndalani. Most of them were ill for a few days. Some were sick for a week. Sometimes, in rare cases, they had to get medicine.

And then, the situation grew worse. Typhoid and malaria became common occurrences. Between five and thirty children had to be taken to the hospital each day to receive emergency medication. Nearly everyone contracted something. At first, the children who got sick from the water adjusted and built an immunity against it. But now, illness had become so pervasive that even the workers left.

Two of the boys had become extremely ill with typhoid. One was taken to the nearby town of Matuu. The other had AIDS, and because of his weakening system they took him to the hospital in Eldoret.

One of the teachers found Charles as he prepared a construction estimate for a girls' dormitory.

"Mr. Mulli?" the teacher asked.

Charles looked up from his work. "Yes?"

"May I come in?"

"Of course. Come in. Sit down."

The teacher stepped into the light, revealing the anxiety on his face. It made Charles fear the worst.

"I have bad news," he said.

Charles put down his pen. "What is it?"

"The sick boy in Matuu is dead."

Charles felt the blood drain from his face.

"The doctors could not save him," the teacher continued. "The water. It gave him a number of illnesses. It was too much for him."

Charles lifted his elbows onto the desk and folded his hands in front of his face. Dead. A child was dead. "Thank you for telling me."

"How is the other boy? The one in Eldoret?"

"I'm going there tomorrow."

"I hope he will make it."

"I do too," Charles said. "I do too."

Charles couldn't sleep. He spent the night in prayer, pleading with God for mercy in healing these children. *God, You see the trouble we are in. You know the child who has died. You know the boy in Eldoret who is also dying. And You know all the children here who are sick. God, You would not have brought us out into this place if You were not also going to provide us with clean water. Would You lead us out of Eldoret all the way to Ndalani only to give us contaminated water? No, God. God, You would not do that. So I plead with You in Jesus' name to bring healing to our family.*

The next morning he drove to the hospital in Eldoret. The doctors warned Charles that the boy did not have much time. Even with the proper medication, the boy's system had already been weakened to the point where the doctors no longer had any solutions for him.

They took Charles to the boy's room. His frail body lay on the bed. A thin blanket covered him. When he saw Charles his eyes lit up, the way children's eyes do when they see their parents.

"Hello," Charles said as he sat down beside him in a chair.

"Daddy. Daddy, I'm so glad to see you again."

"And me, also. I am also glad to see you."

"I'm not feeling well, Daddy. I'm sick. It hurts everywhere." Even in his condition the boy gave Charles a big smile.

"I know it hurts. I'm very sorry that you are sick."

"The doctors have given me medicine. But...but they don't think it will help."

"I know," Charles said, as his eyes filled with tears.

"Can you pray, Daddy? Can you pray for me?"

"Yes, of course I can pray for you."

"I don't have to be afraid, do I?"

"That's right. You do not have to be afraid."

Tears ran down Charles' cheek and fell to the floor. He reached out and placed his left hand on the boy's forehead. With his other hand he lifted the blanket and held the boy's hand.

"I believe in Jesus Christ, Daddy. You told me about Him."

"That's right, I did."

"Do you remember when you found me on the streets?"

"Yes. I remember that very well."

"My parents had died, and I was there in the slums. You brought me to your home. I remember when I first saw you and I thought, I wondered to myself, is he going to pick me? Is he going to take me home with him? And you did." The boy smiled again. "You came up to me, and you said that Jesus loved me. And I know that you love me, too. You gave me a bed. You gave me food. I got to go to your school."

"You did very, very well in school."

"Will I be able to go back?"

Charles wanted to say yes. He wanted to reassure this boy that everything would be all right. It would, of course, be all right.

One way or the other.

"I am so proud of you," Charles said. "You did not go back to the slum. Some of your friends did. They were taken out of the slum and then went back. But you stayed away from the slum and the troubles there. And you sang so well in the choir."

"I love the choir, Daddy."

"Yes, I know that you do."

The boy blinked a number of times as if trying to decide whether to keep his eyes open or closed.

"You are a happy boy," Charles said.

"I am strong in the Lord. That is why I am happy."

"Should we pray?" Charles asked.

The boy nodded his head. They closed their eyes as the boy began to pray.

"Dear Jesus. I know You love me. And I love You. I am sick, and I pray that You will make me better."

The boy's voice trailed off. Charles opened his eyes. The boy opened his, smiled and closed them again.

Charles closed his eyes, forcing out more of the tears. "Father in heaven. I pray for You to heal my dear son and for Your will to be done." Normally, praying came so easy to Charles. It usually felt like he was speaking to someone right beside him. But here in the hospital room he found himself unable to go on.

He felt the boy's hand turn ice-cold. Then his forehead cooled off. Charles opened his eyes. He looked at the young child. His son. His face was so pale. So peaceful. His chest lay motionless. The room went completely still. There was no movement.

Except for the tears on Charles' face.

CHAPTER 30

The entire Eldoret MCF family attended the funeral for the boy. The children had mixed reactions. For some, this was the first person they knew as a friend who had died. For others, it was just another name that would soon be forgotten along with the dozen or so others whom they had already seen die on the streets. Charles officiated at the funeral. And instead of feeling the anger against God that people sometimes feel at funerals for children, Charles focused on how they were going to solve their water problem. God does not make mistakes. He had prayed that morning. Still, it made him wonder how many more children would die before they found a solution to their water problem.

It was too expensive to purify the water. Besides, most purification systems available required electricity, and the MCF site in Ndalani still did not have power. Without power, there was no clean water. And without clean water there was no hope.

Charles prayed to God as he drove the pothole-ridden road from Eldoret to Ndalani. As he crossed the equator, he said, "God, if You don't provide water, please let us go from this place" The idea of a possible move bothered Charles for two reasons. First, they had spent so much energy building the Ndalani site. To go now would mean they would have to rebuild at another location, essentially wasting their efforts and having to start from scratch. Again. Second, the Ndalani location was ideal for the children. It was 100 kilometres away from the city, which separated them from the gangs, prostitution and drugs that lay within the city of Nairobi.

But Charles resolved himself to the idea that leaving might be a possibility and concentrated his prayers on trusting God for financial support to supply water.

Years before, people had suggested digging a well. But according to the history of the area, the numerous attempts that were made to find water ended in failure. The mountains surrounding Ndalani were very dry. Because of the rocky conditions, people were able to dig only seven feet down and found it impossible to obtain water.

The other option was to truck water in. But the demand of 350 children was too great, and the cost associated with supplying water for the children and for their operations was too expensive.

Charles continued praying to God for a solution. For three consecutive nights he was unable to sleep. On the third night, he began to cry as he searched for God's direction. In his small one-bedroom home, he dedicated himself to pursuing an answer from God. The problem was getting worse. More children were getting sick. And the medical costs were adding up.

Charles' crying turned into weeping. His praying escalated from a quiet petition to a loud shout. Pleading, needing, hoping for an answer from God. He knelt before God, his voice growing louder and louder, and lifted his hands to intervene for these children whom God Himself had rescued from the street.

At 1:00 a.m. Esther woke up. She heard Charles shouting as he cried out to the LORD. It scared her. In those vague moments between being in a dream and coming back into reality, she thought at first he was having an argument with someone. When she heard that he was praying, she realized that assumption wasn't too far off.

"Why are you crying like a small baby?" she asked, frustrated at being woken from sleep. "Can't God hear you without you shouting?"

But Charles did not answer. He cried out even louder, struggling with God for an answer on what they should do. His voice was so loud that it hurt Esther's ears to listen to it. It didn't even sound like praying any more.

And then everything went quiet.

There was a dramatic shift in the atmosphere of the room. Charles felt a sudden peace and an undeniable conviction that a solution had been found.

"What?" Esther whispered.

Again, Charles made no response. He stayed there on his knees, his head arched back, his face looking up. The moonlight coming in through the opening revealed his tear-soaked shirt. It was so wet that it looked like heavy perspiration.

"Charles," she said again. "What is it?"

He opened his eyes. That familiar fire was in them again.

"Let's go out and find where God has given us water."

"What?"

Charles got up and took his wife by the hand and led her to the door.

"Water, Esther. God has given us water."

Charles opened the door. He walked, with her right behind him, as though he was following some invisible map. From their small home with the cracked walls and leaking roof, they walked 200 metres to the west. Esther followed him, wondering how on earth he knew where he was going. He stopped. She nearly bumped into him. Charles moved three metres to the side.

"This is it," he said.

They were standing a long distance away from the river and far from any of the dormitories.

"This is what?" Esther asked.

"This is where God has given us water."

"Here?"

Charles turned to look at her. "Right here, my wife."

"Here?"

"Yes."

"Right here?"

He smiled. "Esther, you are going to see a miracle. We don't need to see it with our eyes. I've seen it in my spirit. This is where it is."

Esther looked at the parched ground. People had studied this area for years. There was no water. It was impossible. That's what they said.

"All right," she replied. "We have water."

Charles grabbed a handful of soil. Esther did the same.

"Father, we stand here because You have shown us that You are our provider. You have provided water for us right here. Everybody says there is no water, but You say there is. So my precious wife and I are here to dedicate this well for Your work, so that the children might have clean water."

They opened their eyes. Esther laughed. "So I'm standing on a well?"

"Exactly. You are standing on the future water supply of MCF in Ndalani."

They walked back to their home, and Charles had the best night's sleep in a long time.

The next day, Charles assembled all the children together. They crowded around the place where Charles and Esther had stood the night before. They sang a song, and then Charles told them why they were here.

"I have not been able to sleep for quite a while. All of you know that we have a terrible problem here in Ndalani. We have no clean water. And so we have been praying to our God to do a miracle for us. Do you believe that? Do you believe that God still does miracles for His children?"

The children shouted out that they agreed God still did miracles. It wasn't just a platitude. Most of them had seen miracles firsthand. Demonic deliverance. Healing. Salvation.

"So God showed me this spot. Out of all the places here at MCF Ndalani, God showed me to dig right here. And today we are going to pray for the workers, that God will bless them as they begin to dig. Now we don't have many expensive tools here at MCF. But remember the story of Moses? Who here remembers the story of Moses?"

Most of the children raised their hands.

"When Moses stood before God, he was worried that Pharaoh would not listen to him. So God said, 'What do you have in your hand?' And Moses told God that he had a staff. And God changed it into a snake. What God was doing was telling Moses that He would use the things Moses already had in his possession to deliver the people of Egypt. Moses had faith; he had a staff and he had his brother, Aaron. We have faith, our small tools and our willing workers. God will provide for us, too"

They prayed for two hours. The children took turns praying out loud. Some of them were used to getting up at 5:00 a.m. and praying in the classrooms for an hour before the day started. They prayed so loud that people across the property, about a city block away, could hear them shouting to God. Now their prayers rose up to God, thanking Him in advance for the success of the workers.

They started digging that morning. They made a hole about 2 metres by 3 metres wide and spent three days in the unforgiving sun removing the soil. On the fourth day, they had gone down the depth of a two-storey house and hit rock. The workers were exhausted, and finding nothing but rock at the bottom made them want to give up. Off to the side at the bottom of the hole they noticed a soft, yellowish clay. They struck their shovels against it.

Then they heard a sound of rumbling under the ground.

Water shot up through the opening, the way water explodes out of a fire hydrant that has been knocked down by a car. The workers raced up the ladder. Children nearby ran throughout the site yelling, "*Maji! Maji Maji!*"

Charles was outside his office and heard them screaming as they ran towards him, telling him they had found water. Charles called for Esther, and together they went to the site. They looked down the hole and saw the bubbling water.

The impossible had become reality.

Charles went to Nairobi to buy pumps and had them installed at the site. They gathered the children together and named the place Jacob's Well. Charles explained that even as people in the Bible could get water from Jacob's well, so all of MCF could come and get clean water without cost.

Later that evening, after all the children had gone to bed, Charles and Esther came back to the new well.

"This has helped all of us believe that God is able to answer prayer," Esther said.

"The children are encouraged. Now, when they pass this well on the way to school each morning, they will remember that God did a miracle."

"The water is good," Esther said. "God gave us clean water."

"And He's going to do much, much more."

A missionary from overseas wrote Charles, saying he had heard about MCF and wanted to visit him. Charles picked him up from Nairobi and took him to the Ndalani site.

"You don't have any electricity?" the missionary asked.

"No, we are still waiting for power."

"I will see what can be done about that."

A month later the missionary wrote again to say he was so impressed with MCF that he wanted to set up electrical lines for them from the main grid. Charles wrote back thanking him for his compassion and willingness to act in a tangible way. Charles prepared a budget and also expressed the need for a second well.

Within a year, two development partners of MCF had supplied all the money for the electricity requirements and the bore hole for an extra well.

When the lights went on, the children celebrated late into the evening with a thanksgiving service. God had provided water, and God had provided light.

"These are manifestations of His love and promise to His people," Charles said. "We are so thankful for our many friends who live outside of Kenya. We have friends all around the world—in North America, in Europe, in Australia, in Israel and in other places—and although they are far away, they are part of our Mully Children's Family. Last year we did not have clean water. We did not have lights, so we could not have programs in the evening. But God listened to our prayers. He provided. Today we have clean water and we have lights. God listens to the prayers of His people."

CHAPTER 31

MCF faced constant challenges on a daily basis. There were the obvious ones—the ones people visiting the site could see—like the need for better dormitories and sleeping arrangements, for more school textbooks, for food supplies. But then there were the unseen problems. These were problems visitors rarely saw, which, for the most part, was a good thing. But the MCF family, especially Charles' biological children, were not spared the unseen world. For them it was more real than the visible one. And when it manifested itself, the spiritually-in-tune at MCF were called upon to deal with these horrific situations.

His name was Kikoi, and he came from a Muslim background. His divorced parents were from Ethiopia, but he lived with his mother, who moved from the tourist city of Mombassa to Eldoret. She became a prostitute, forcing Kikoi and his brothers to live on the street. They had to fight for their existence by whatever means they could and use every method at their disposal to survive.

At age eight, Kikoi had killed a boy.

There had been an argument over something. Food probably. Whatever it was, Kikoi hated the boy. He had stolen a knife from one of the stores. One evening, in the pouring rain, he walked up behind the boy and stabbed him. The child's body jerked back as he absorbed the impact. He fell to the ground on his back. Kikoi looked at the boy, who no doubt wondered why he was dying at the hands of a person he hardly knew. Kikoi just watched as the life faded out of the boy's eyes.

Charles found Kikoi in the slums in 1994 and brought him to MCF Ndalani. He started in the school program and got to know some of the other students. It wasn't long before he took an unhealthy interest in a young girl named Sarah. When she walked to class alone, he pushed her and bothered her, calling her names. She didn't know why he did it and, trying to ignore it, decided not to tell any of her friends what was happening.

Day after day this went on, and Sarah became increasingly distressed. When she went to sleep at night, she saw terrible visions. She saw an unidentifiable man chasing after her. Sometimes he wanted to strangle her. Other times he held a particular knife in his hand while he tried to hunt her down and kill her. These nightmares never left her. Each evening they were there to terrify her when she drifted off to sleep.

She learned to check behind her whenever she was going to class alone. She avoided eye contact with Kikoi. Whenever she saw him approaching, she turned and walked the other way. But that only made matters worse.

He chased after her and threatened to force her to sleep with him. She refused him and, plagued by an inseparable mixture of guilt and fear, also refused to seek help.

One evening, she was heading off to the classroom to join her friends in a mandatory study period. Just as she was about to enter, Kikoi snuck up behind her. He grabbed her and turned her away from the door. His eyes were only half open. He clenched his teeth.

"If you do not sleep with me, I will kill you!"

From behind his back he pulled out a knife. She recognized it. It was the knife from her dreams.

She screamed. Kikoi released his hold on her and ran off. The students rushed outside and saw her standing there, crying, wishing she could leave MCF and her nightmares behind.

Charles came and took her to the open area outside the primary classrooms. They sat down among the flowers and trees. She looked over her shoulder, thinking that at any moment Kikoi might come back to finish her off.

"Sarah. Tell me what happened."

She got only the first few sentences out. That was enough for Charles. He called some of the teachers to bring Kikoi so they could question him.

Mulwa, Kamau, Omolo, and more than a dozen others brought Kikoi to Charles. He stood in silence before them. Sarah stood beside

Charles. But the longer she looked at Kikoi, the more she moved behind Charles, as if to do everything possible to distance herself from him.

"Kikoi, do you know this girl?"

Kikoi said nothing.

Charles asked again. "Do you know this girl?"

He then turned to Sarah and asked her to explain what happened. She did. Kikoi listened to all of it, not giving any indication whether he agreed or disagreed.

"Is this true?" Charles asked him.

Still no answer from Kikoi.

Charles was about to ask him again when Kikoi let out a blood-curdling scream. With super-human strength Kikoi jumped up above their heads and in one dramatic motion turned his body horizontal in the air. The setting sun revealed a crazed look in his eyes as he hovered there. He slowly lowered himself to the ground, screaming unholy sounds on his descent.

When he landed sideways on the ground, he began to spin around at an unnatural pace, like a wheel being whipped around in circles by an unseen force. Wild screams shot out from him.

Sarah shrilled. Her high-pitched scream, though, was no match for the shouts coming from Kikoi.

Charles stood up and shouted, "In the name of Jesus Christ, we refuse all the evil spirits!"

Kamau and Omolo made the mistake of trying to grab Kikoi. They reached down to take hold of his arms. Kikoi got up and flung them off, making them look like nothing more than rag dolls. Kamau and Omolo crashed to the ground. Kikoi kicked a nearby chair with such force that it flew farther than any normal human being could manage.

Mulwa came to help, as did more than twenty others. All of them together could not contain Kikoi. He screamed and shouted, smacking people away with effortless moves. He spoke in languages none of them had ever heard.

The twenty men tried again, this time with ropes. They managed to bind his arms and legs, leaving him a twitching, howling anomaly on the ground.

This is really the devil, Charles thought. He went to get his Bible and Dickson, his only biological child at Ndalani at the time, who had significant experience and power in casting out demons. "Dickson!" Charles shouted as he came to his room. "Get your Bible. Kikoi needs our help."

The look of determination in Charles' eyes told Dickson that whatever they were about to encounter would either match or exceed anything they had experienced to date.

When they came back to the area, they saw that Kikoi had stopped moving. He wasn't yelling any more and wasn't speaking in any strange languages. Kikoi later told them that he had once forecast that twenty-six people would die in a bus accident. And the next day it had happened.

"Take the ropes off him," Charles said.

"What?" one of them asked.

"Take the ropes off him. You can not bind the devil with ropes."

They took the ropes off, fearing for their lives as they did so.

Charles, Dickson and two others took turns praying for over five hours. They read passages from the Bible, citing numerous verses, including those where Jesus had cast out demons. Then Charles laid his hands on him.

"Father God. You see the trouble that Kikoi is in. But Father, we know that You are much more powerful. You are stronger. No evil force can come against You. So in the name of Jesus Christ I command these demons to leave, and I pray now for Kikoi to be delivered from this darkness."

Charles took his hands off him. All four looked at Kikoi, wondering what was going to happen. Kikoi did nothing for the first while. Then he stood up and staggered like a drunken man.

"In the name of Jesus Christ the demons must leave!"

As soon as Charles touched him a second time, Kikoi crumpled to the ground. They gathered around him again, praying and quoting verses. His eyes opened and closed. Like a lethargic patient recovering from an operation, he tried to speak but found no words. For two hours Kikoi could not say the name Jesus.

"Kikoi," Charles said. "You are free. You are free in Jesus' name. You are no longer bound by the demons. Do you realize this?"

Nothing.

"Kikoi. Who has freed you?"

Still nothing.

"Kikoi. Who has taken away the terror of those demons and made you free?"

Kikoi sat up. His eyes looked better—still hazy, but much better than the bewildered look of evil that was there only a few hours earlier.

"Jesus has freed me," Kikoi said. "Jesus Christ has set me free."

The men watched him the entire night. The next day a number of them fasted and prayed for the demonic forces to stay away. Kikoi began to read the Bible and stayed in regular communication with God. He never had another attack.

"You did well, Dickson," Charles said as the father-son team walked back to their rooms, exhausted. "I can count on you. On all of my children. I can count on you for the small things and the great things. I am proud of you."

Dickson gave his father a hug, realizing only then how tired he really was.

"These experiences make us stronger," Charles said. "Always be prepared for the evil day. And never be afraid to confront it."

CHAPTER 32

She shouldn't have been walking alone.

It was dark. It was late. And although she didn't realize it, she was breathing heavily through her mouth. Every step she took on the muddy road seemed louder than it was. She tried not to make eye contact with the men who were staring at her slender teenage body. But it did little to help. Those sickening eyes bored holes into her as she walked faster and faster. It wouldn't take much. All they would have to do is reach out and grab her. They would have their way with her and throw her bruised body back into the streets. She would cry. She would scream. But it wouldn't matter. Not here.

Not for a young girl named Rael Wanjuki in the Huruma slums in Eldoret.

One of them called out to her. Her body shot out a burst of adrenaline with such force that it nearly choked her. He called out again and asked how much. He laughed, and she wondered if he was gaining ground. She broke into a jog. "How much?" he shouted again. She wanted to look behind her. She wanted to see how close he was, but somehow, not knowing gave her the only hope she could find.

"How much?"

She started running. His cackling laugh came closer. She ran as fast as she could. Her eyes darted along the side of the road for some place familiar to seek refuge. *How much?*

Her foot slammed into a pothole. Her body jerked forward as she fell to the ground. Filthy water splashed onto her face. She crawled trying to get back to her feet, fearing that at any moment those powerful hands would take hold of her as she lay there helpless in the middle of the road.

She got back up. The pulse in her neck pounded with such intensity that it echoed in her ears. He was right there. Right behind her. She felt his presence bearing down on her. Rael screamed. She turned around and braced herself for the onslaught. She fell on her back and looked into the black night, waiting for her attacker to appear.

But the road was empty.

The night quiet.

There was no one there.

Not this time.

She lay in the putrid, disease-ridden puddles, trying to calm down and convince herself that everything she had heard and felt was just her imagination. This would normally be the time when a teenage girl would cry. It would normally be the time when fearing the worst and being relieved that it had not happened would produce some kind of a response. But this was the slum. This was her life. And the hopelessness of her few years of subsistence in this unforgiving world had already taught her the futility of tears.

She made it down the street to her family's one-room rented house without hearing anything more along the way. She lived with her mother, her four brothers and her three sisters. She didn't know her dad. None of them did. They had all been fathered by different men.

Rael was about to put her hand on the door handle when she heard those familiar sounds. She cringed. A wave of disgust came over her. The grunts of some stranger inside filled the small house and seeped out to Rael's ears. She closed her eyes and felt the insecurity that came with realizing she was no better off in the house than on the streets. Her mother was at work again. Doing what she knew, to make what pathetic little money she could for herself, and leaving even less for her starving family.

Rael waited on the ground at the door to the house in that shaky world between a danger she was all too familiar with and a danger she was only beginning to understand. The night seemed to go on forever. Not that it mattered. Not to Rael. Today was the same as yesterday, which would be the same as tomorrow, and the same as the day after that and the day after that. There was no such thing as time in the slum. Life was one big repeat in the worst part of the world.

When it was over, a man opened the door. If he saw Rael half asleep slumped against the wall, he gave no indication that it made any difference to him. The seven children who had been in the same room with him and their mother hadn't bothered him; hence, a girl stranded out in the street because of him would make little impact. He left the door open as he walked down the street and disappeared in the blackness of night.

She stood up. Her legs were sore from sitting too long. Even though he was gone, her mind replayed the sounds she had heard tonight and the hundreds she had heard over previous nights. She walked in the door, and the second she closed it behind her, she knew what was coming.

It was the smell that gave it away. That stabbing odour of the illicit *changa'a* brew her mother cooked and drank to rid herself of the guilt and awareness of her deplorable condition. Sometimes she sold it. But most times she wasn't able to part with it. Especially not tonight.

Rael saw her brothers and sisters lying on the ground pretending not to have heard anything, pretending not to have noticed, pretending to be asleep so as not to face their drunken mother.

"You," Rael's mother said. "Why do you come back here?" She had a crazed look in her eyes. She sucked back on the drink. Rael caught another waft of it, bringing tears to her eyes.

"Why do you stay here?" Her voice got louder. Her skin grew paler. She took a step towards Rael, then stumbled to the side. She would have fallen had the wall not been there to stop her. She stayed there a moment, pinned against the rickety metal siding, looking as though she was about to pass out. That would have been good. Among the three options of being out on the street with rapists, in the house with a violent, drunk mother, or being in a house with a violent but unconscious drunk mother, it was the latter Rael always hoped for.

Her mother sucked back another mouthful of toxin and stood up straight. "Don't you get it? How could you be so stupid, you rotten, filthy animal?" Spit dribbled out the side of her mouth as she shouted. "I don't want you here! I don't want any of you here!"

Her mother scanned the room, eying those costly dependents. Then she screamed with such ferocity that it jolted some of the children out of their fake sleep. "I don't want any of you here! I hate you! I hate every single one of you! You know what all of you are! You know where you come from! You are nothing! Nothing!"

Her two younger siblings began to cry. The five older siblings said nothing. They knew the drill. Rael stood her ground. Her mother looked at her and squinted her eyes. "You pathetic child." She stepped closer to Rael and then bent down to be at her level. They looked into each other's eyes. Rael saw death. Her mother saw nothing. "Whether you live or die makes no difference to me."

Rael would have assumed this was the alcohol talking had she not often heard those same words from her mother when she was sober.

With speed that surprised even Rael, her mother lunged out at her and smashed the palm of her hand across her face. The blow spun Rael around, sending her crashing to the ground, much like when she fell in that pothole. The other children cried louder. The mother finished her drink and stumbled to the door. That deadly sound of the lock clicking into place spelled horror for all the children. She walked back to Rael, who had curled up in the corner. She kicked her in the ribs, spit on her, and then proceeded to beat each child in succession.

The screams and cries of the children filled the room and carried out into the streets. But there was no one to help. There never was.

Those in nearby houses had similar problems of their own.

There was no money for food, clothing or schooling. Sometimes her mother was sent to jail for up to two weeks at a time for brewing the illegal *changa'a*. This forced the children to go to sleep hungry and to beg for food. Rael's older brothers and sisters ran away to the streets to fend for themselves, a dangerous prospect but one that provided a better means of finding food than living in the same house as their mother. Some of the older sisters later got married and felt the joy of having a new start. But their optimism was soon replaced with the same desperation with which they had grown up. Their husbands were also poor, forcing them to live with the constant question of when, or if, there would be food or a future.

"We have to go, too," Rael said to her younger brother.

"To the streets?"

"Do you really want to stay here?"

They were alone in the house. Their mother was gone. At work.

"Of course not. But where will we go?"

"What difference does it make? We'll be better off there than here. Do you want to starve?"

"No."

"Well?"

"You're sure about this?"

"No."

"Then why are you doing it?"

"Because I'm not taking another beating here," Rael said. "Maybe it will be better on the streets. Maybe it will be worse. But at least there will be something to eat. I'm not sitting here and starving. That's what we have to look forward to if we don't go."

"You know what happens on the streets. You know how people get money. Is that what you want?"

"Do you want to stay here and die? Is that what you want?"

"You don't know what life will be like."

"Yes, I do. I'm going to find people who love me. I'm going to find people who will help me get food. I'm going to find a good home to live in. And we're going to have freedom. We can do what we want. Go where we want. And be with whomever we want. This is a dream come true. It's all out there waiting for us. All we have to do is go out there and grab it."

Her brother thought for a moment. He looked up at her. She showed no sign of hesitation. "All right," he said. "Let's go."

She led the way out of the house. They left the door open. They would not be coming back.

The streets were not what Rael had hoped for. After only a few days of their would-be adventure, she was separated from her brother. The boys had their gang, and the girls had theirs. Initiation was the hardest. The girls beat Rael and insulted her. But her mother had trained her well, and so Rael found herself able to stand against it. Within weeks a girls' gang took her into their fold.

She suffered from diarrhea and brutal stomach ailments that resulted from having to dig for food in garbage bins. Behind restaurants, in people's backyards and outside stores, Rael pulled back garbage can lids and reached inside the sloppy guck of waste looking for anything to eat.

Rael slept with her gang friends on verandas. Security men often chased them away or beat and raped them. From street to street and garbage bin to garbage bin, Rael travelled around the city of Eldoret with her gang, trying to find a way to live.

In order to get money, Rael joined the rest of the girls in prostitution. It wasn't hard. There was lots of opportunity. Her friends showed her how it was done. They went to bars and discos and found men who paid them a pittance for sex. Some clients got violent and beat Rael. They were the worst. The best were the ones who got drunk. These were the ones Rael and her friends could steal from when they passed out.

But with the decision to enter into prostitution came the accompanying guilt. She'd seen this before. And try as she could, Rael wasn't able to avoid the reality that she was turning into her mother. To cope with the disparity, Rael turned to drugs. The money she made from prostitution was supposed to go for better food. It rarely got spent that way. Food could come and go, but it couldn't bring about peace of mind. Drugs did that. At least for the time being. The down side was that they left a nasty addiction problem. What was once just a means of escape, just an attempt to be a kid again, turned into a never-ending quest for satisfaction.

More need of drugs meant more need of money, which meant more prostitution. After getting the money and the drugs, Rael sometimes hung out in a quiet alley, away from the world, getting high and feeling the temporary relief that came with not having to think about anything. But when the drugs wore off and she came back from whatever world she had visited, she felt the depression that came with knowing there was no way out.

Prostitution. Drugs. Rape. Rotten food. No place to sleep.

Rael was living a street child's dream.

It was May 1993 when she saw Charles for the first time. She had heard about him from some of the other children. She had never seen him. All she knew was that he was some rich man who gave his money away to help street children.

When she saw him and two other men coming towards her, she worried about their intent.

"*Ooo-aye,*" Charles said.

Rael said nothing. Men couldn't be trusted. Charles came closer.

"How are you?" Charles asked.

She looked at him, trying to figure out what he was doing here. He was unlike anyone she'd ever seen before. His clothes were normal. Medium height. Medium build. But those eyes. There was something about his eyes.

"My name is Charles Mulli."

Something inside Rael sparked when she heard that. It was him. Charles Mulli.

The legend.

He reached out his hand and offered it to Rael. She looked at her friends for support, and finding no disagreement in their expressions she shook his hand. It was warm.

"How did you come to be on the street?" he asked.

His eyes were honest. She felt she could see right through them into his soul. She told him her story, the short version, and wondered what his motive was in coming to talk with them. There was something different about him. It was as though an aura of passion radiated from him and had somehow managed to envelope her. She'd never felt love before. Lust, yes. Love, no. So when it showed up at her doorstep, she wasn't able to recognize it.

He talked to the girls for a while, telling them who he was and what he did.

"I want to tell you that Jesus loves you," he said. "He loves you so much." He told them about his childhood, or lack thereof, how God had changed his life and how God could change their lives, too.

It was hard for Rael to believe. If there really was a God who loved her then why was she on the streets? Why did God let her suffer at the hands of those countless men? Why did she have such a brutal mother? Why did she have to escape to the streets?

Charles took the girls to a nearby store and bought them food. He talked about the home where girls like them got a new start. He talked about how God saved his life and how they, too, could be saved, not just from the streets but from their lives.

"I want to invite you to come and live with me. I want you to be my children. What do you say?"

She didn't know about the home. She didn't know about God. And she didn't know about Charles. But she knew the street, and she knew she had long since reached the end. Escaping from her violent mother to the streets was worth a try. Perhaps going with Charles was worth a try.

"All right," she said. "I'll come."

She and five other girls from the gang got into Charles' car. She closed the door behind her. Rael was starting a new life.

Rael had a father.

When she arrived at the Mully Children's Family home in Eldoret, she met Esther. Sometimes strangers meet and it feels as though they have known each other their whole lives. That's how it felt when Rael met Esther. They sat down. As they talked, Rael felt what it was like to have someone listen to her without wanting something from her. She felt the first inkling of what it was like to have a real mother.

A mother who wasn't drunk. A mother who didn't chase her away. A mother who had the same genuine love for her as her new-found father had.

She took a shower. It was the first time she had ever been in a good bathroom. Afterwards, Esther brought her new clothes and introduced her to the family. She saw the myriad of new faces as children came up to greet her. Two of the faces in the distance looked familiar. She recognized them. They had grown up. They looked different from the images she had burned in her memory from when she had last seen them. Sure enough. It was them.

Her younger brother and her younger sister.

When they saw her they broke through the crowd and clutched onto her. Rael started crying. The other children ran off and continued on with their games, shouting as they left. But the three of them stayed together. Reunited. This time they had more siblings.

And both a father and a mother.

Even though MCF had given her the dream of a lifetime, Rael ran away from the Mullis and returned to the streets. The addictions to drugs and sex were hard, if not impossible, to leave behind. Returning to where she had come from seemed, at times, to be the perfect answer to her struggles. While back on the street, she found herself wondering why she was doing the very things she did not want to do. They were wrong. They were destroying her. She knew this. Yet she was powerless to get rid of them.

Every time a child ran away, Charles went out looking for them. Most of the time he found them and talked with them. He would bring them back, only to have them run back to the street and start the process all over again.

"Rael!" Charles called out from the window of his car. Finally, he had found her. It was pouring rain. She did not hear him.

"Rael!" Charles called again. He opened the door and walked after her. "Rael! It's me! Your daddy."

Rael turned around. She looked sick. Her face was pale. Her eyes were all screwed up.

"Rael," Charles said, seeing the desperation in her face. "I'm here to take you home."

"What's the matter with you?" she snapped. They'd been here before. "Nobody wants me. Nobody! Not you. Not anyone. Why do you keep coming after me?"

She turned and walked away.

"Because I love you, Rael."

She stopped walking. They stood there in the deluge, not saying anything. She turned around. She was crying. Even with the rain pounding on her face, the tears were impossible to miss.

"Nobody loves me."

"I love you. Your mother loves you. And God loves you the most of all. Come home, Rael. You have a very big family at home. You have so many brothers and sisters. We love you."

She felt the stupidity of what she had done and realized the futility of being back to this dump of a lifestyle on the streets. Charles walked up to her and gave her a hug.

"I don't want to be here," she cried.

"I know that you don't. And I'm here to bring you back."

"Why do I do this?"

"It's okay, Rael. We're going home."

"Why do I do this, Daddy? Why do I run away?"

"It's going to be all right. Can I take you home?"

She nodded her head.

Through the example of Charles and Esther Mulli and the daily devotionals and Bible studies at the school, Rael saw and learned about Christ. In 1997, she surrendered her life to Jesus. That same year she moved to the Ndalani property with numerous other children.

Two years later, she made a trip from Ndalani to Eldoret with her brother and sister to visit their ailing mother. She was suffering from her long bout with alcohol. The closer they got to Eldoret, the more intense her childhood memories became. It was as though some magnet was drawing her into the past to relive the abuse and abandonment. But seeing her mother would give her a chance to talk through the hardships they had been through and reconcile their sordid history with one another.

In 2001, Rael received a letter saying her mother had passed away. It was expected, at least to some degree; still, Rael felt the loss of her birth mother. Esther told Rael that her mother had given her life to Christ before she had died. It gave Rael the comfort she needed to know that one of her biological parents would be in heaven when she got there.

Her mother's extended family refused to pay for any of the hospital bills, rental arrears or funeral expenses, so Charles paid them on her behalf. The medical tests revealed she had died of HIV/AIDS.

CHAPTER 33

Back at Ndalani, Rael found it difficult to concentrate in class. She attended numerous counselling sessions and prayer meetings, where Charles, Esther and other social workers encouraged her. But the effects of her past were difficult to overcome, and there was this sinister impulse to return to her old life. She faked an illness and was taken to Eldoret for treatment. There, she stole money from one of the teachers and travelled to Mombassa, where she could be away from everyone she knew.

She found accommodations with a woman she met and resorted to a familiar way of earning money. She worked as a prostitute in Mombassa for more than a year. By that time she was emaciated, having dropped from 67 kilograms (142 pounds) down to 25 kilograms (55 pounds). She returned to Eldoret and sought refuge with an aunt, who wanted nothing to do with her. Having no other recourse, Rael began the twenty kilometre walk to MCF, hoping the Mullis would once again take her back.

Every step felt like a marathon. Every breath like it would be her last. Her lungs felt the sting of exhaustion. Her body was weak with illness. She refused to believe what everyone had told her, that she was dying of a disease that had no cure. She didn't want to believe it. Maybe not believing could prevent it from being true.

She collapsed on the road only 200 metres from MCF. She fell asleep, and by good fortune, or design, a passerby came to check on her. Some people from MCF came and took her home. A week later, Charles and Esther came up from Ndalani to see her. They took her to the hospital, where she was diagnosed with tuberculosis and HIV/AIDS.

In the months to come, Rael regained weight while struggling with HIV/AIDS. She went on to college and majored in adolescent and peer counselling, with the hope of being able to counsel those around her, as well as her brothers and sisters in MCF. Her hope was to help them so that they would not find themselves in the same mess she found herself in.

Of the numerous events in her life that Rael thought about, Charles and Esther's unconditional acceptance was the one she reflected on most often. When she was thrown out, they took her in. When others took advantage of her, they gave their lives for her. When everyone else rejected her, they held their arms open wide—even when she proved time and again she wasn't worthy of being taken back.

Which is probably why she understood Christ so well.

Life for Daniel Mbisi was both crowded and empty.

His mother had thirteen children from a variety of relationships. At the time, the man she was living with was her fifth husband. A younger brother and sister died of malnutrition and lack of medical care. Some of the older siblings ran off to the streets in a vain attempt at finding something better than what they had at home. Still, the house was jam-packed with children who had come from a variety of mother-father combinations.

But even in a house filled with people a person can feel desperate and alone.

Such was the case for six-year-old Daniel.

His mother's wages as a prostitute and her meagre income selling illegal, homemade alcohol were hardly enough to provide for the family. His stepfather worked as a casual labourer, earning little more than what was needed to look after himself. Food was hard to come by. Medical attention was scarce. Education was nonexistent.

Daniel's stepfather loved only his biological children, which created a rift of hatred in the family. Siblings didn't speak to each other. Some considered themselves rightful children. Others, like Daniel, were looked on as extra expenses that dragged the rest of the family down.

Daniel lived in the Munyaka slum in Eldoret. During the day he worked odd jobs where all the money he earned went to the family. After a day of doing whatever he could to earn a place in the family, he came home on an empty stomach to a drunk mother and father. He could hear the yelling as he came towards their crammed house. Kids screaming at each other. Parents at the kids. The kids at the parents.

He opened the door. And that was when his day went from bad to worse.

"Where is it?" his stepfather yelled from his chair. He didn't even look at his son. His stepson.

Daniel held out his hand. A small coin. A pathetic amount, really. Even for a slum. His stepfather turned to look at him. His expression went from anger to hatred. In that moment, the familiar feeling of worthlessness in the presence of his stepfather overwhelmed him.

"That's it? That's all you brought?"

"I worked all day. This is everything."

"It's not good enough!"

He got up from the chair. Daniel hurried to get out. Even though he had never outran his father to the door, he hung on to the optimism that there was always a chance. But today would be no different. His stepfather smacked him in the head from behind. Daniel spun around and fell to the ground. His shoulders hit the ground first. Then his head followed as it snapped back. His stepfather yelled at him, but Daniel couldn't hear it. All he could see was this towering figure above him, screaming at him while the world became blurry from the pain at the base of his skull.

What followed next was routine. More yelling. More pushing. Then Daniel's mother got in on the action. Husband number five was no worse than the others. They all suffered from the same intolerable influence of evil. When Daniel tried to stand up, his drunk mother whacked him. The blow came more into his face than across it, feeling more like a punch than a slap. The force of the heel of her hand against his forehead sent him sprawling backwards. His spine crashed into the corner of the wall. He dropped to the ground, not from the pain but in the knowledge of how to survive these attacks. If he was on the ground, they wouldn't hit him. It was considered a mercy rule. So to speak.

They left him there and went back to their drinking and shouting. Daniel lay on the floor, saying nothing. Crying a little. But not as much as he used to. There was no point.

There never was.

The next morning Daniel made the decision to run away from home. The choice was simply, really. Abuse, no food, no education, no clothing. There was nothing. He was nothing. At least that's how he felt living at home. Perhaps things would be better on the streets. Perhaps the world out there would be kinder than the world inside his parents' house.

Or, perhaps, it would be much, much worse.

In his first week, Daniel drank the disease-infested water of the Sosiani River. Even though it tasted awful, it helped, in the short term, to curb the starvation pangs in his guts. A week without food for a small boy can feel like dying.

And in many ways, he was.

His first impression of the city of Eldoret was that he had found his ticket to the good life. Tall buildings. Sleek cars. People wearing nice clothes. People working. He assumed everyone living in the streets could acquire this lifestyle.

He spent his first day searching for food. He found none, except for the slimy remains in garbage cans. He took off the lids, reached inside and pulled up a mixture of soggy bread and rotten lettuce that had a strange brown-purple colour to it. He closed his eyes and stuffed it in his mouth. He didn't throw up. Didn't even gag. It was better than starving.

He joined a group of boys. who took them into their gang. They started him on cigarettes and marijuana and taught him how to survive. They stole from stores and people on the streets. Slept wherever they could. Took drugs. It was life on the street. It was the Eldoret dream.

Over the next six years, Daniel graduated to the tougher drugs like heroin, opium and cocaine. The teenage boys trained twelve-year-old Daniel to be an asset in their criminal activities. He entered people's houses through a window and opened the door for the rest of the gang to enter. They also used him to smuggle drugs. He was perfect. The police never suspected him at such a young age. The gang paid him in drugs. It was the currency of their trade.

He tried to trade the drugs for money wherever possible in order to buy food. But that was tough to do. Selling drugs was a competitive market. Often, he consumed the drugs as a reliable, if not consequential, means of ridding his conscience of the guilt over who he had become and the things he was doing to other people and to himself. That left him to hunt the garbage bins in search of soggy bread, rotten lettuce and whatever else he could find.

While the police had a hard time catching up with Daniel, the people in the community did not. There were two types of justice. Legal justice administered by the police and mob justice administered by the locals. The former was overbearing.

But the latter was life-threatening.

Stealing was a way of life for Daniel. Bakeries. Stores. People on the streets. He excelled in the art of pickpocketing. But on some occasions he wasn't good enough. On some occasions he got careless. And on some occasions the public taught him what they thought of his thievery.

He had stolen from a man who had just come out of a store. Daniel reached into the man's bag from behind and pulled out a small package. In and of itself, it was hardly worth the impending punishment. The man noticed before Daniel could put the package under his shirt. He reached out to grab him. Daniel pulled back. The man lunged again, but by now Daniel had enough of a lead on him. The man yelled out and pointed to Daniel.

"Stop that street boy! He has stolen from me!"

Daniel ran as fast as he could. Three young men nearby gave chase. They screamed as they raced after him. "Stop that street boy! He has stolen!"

What began with three people turned into a dozen. People who had no connection to the incident were now bearing down on him to inflict justice—their version of justice—on him. People standing on the street were just a blur to Daniel as he raced by them. He couldn't remember what street he was on. He looked for a familiar sign or store but recognized nothing. He'd been here so many times. He had stolen from all of these stores. How was it that his state of panic had left him unable to find a suitable hiding spot?

He turned a corner, and the moment he did so he knew he was in serious trouble. There in front of him was a brick wall, and stores on either side. How could he have been so careless? He wanted to turn back the other way. But the moment he spun around he saw his pursuers enter the alley. There were even more of them now. People had joined the cause to get him. There were too many of them. He wouldn't be able to fight them. Not even if his whole gang was here could they take on these citizens-turned-mercenaries.

"You have stolen, street boy!" a man shouted in a loud voice.

They came closer. Daniel backed up against the brick wall. He saw their angry eyes. He saw their clenched hands. He took a deep breath.

And wondered if it would be his last.

A fist flew out of the air and crashed into his nose. The bright day turned black. Everything went quiet. It seemed as if everything was happening in slow motion. He stumbled backwards from the blow much like he had when his stepfather or mother struck him. But instead of falling, he managed to keep his balance. He should have fallen. He should have remembered the lesson he learned when he was growing up.

The next fist landed clear across his face, catching him both in his cheekbone and his teeth. He heard a crack. Then he felt a tug at his shoulders as someone pulled him forward. He raised his hands to protect his face and felt a pounding blow to his stomach. The mob formed a circle around him. They screamed at him. "You worthless fool! You are nothing! Nothing!" Someone grabbed him from behind and threw him across the ring. He tripped and fell. Just as his face came crashing to the ground, a foot smashed into his jaw. His teeth slammed together. His head snapped back and then came crashing down on a stone, splitting his chin open. Feet kicked away at him, piercing into his bony ribs. They spit on him. Stomped on him. One person took a stick and whipped his back and buttocks. He curled up as best he could. At first everything hurt. But as the blood started coming out of his mouth and nose, and as the blows to his head sent him into unconsciousness, the pain began to subside.

They stopped beating him when they saw he wasn't moving any more. No twitch. No moaning. No plea for help. He was done. They were done. One less problem. One less thief. One less pathetic street child.

It was evening when Daniel opened his eyes. Everything was dark. Everything hurt. He tried to open his mouth, but his jaw refused to move. His ribs ached. His back was full of bruises. Dried blood covered his face. He wanted to get up, but his body would not respond. So he stayed there. In the alley. Cold. Hungry. Hurting.

Alone.

Daniel's gang found him later that evening. By this time his face had turned a deep black. His cheeks had swelled up so much it looked as if he had an entire apple in his mouth. He needed a hospital. That much was obvious to all of them. But they had no money, and they had no contacts to get him there. So they gave him the only two medications they had. Marijuana and heroin. Sure, when the drugs wore off he'd have to deal with the pain again, and not just the physical pain. The bruises, the cuts, the breaks—his body would heal. The real problem was the inner pain—the hopelessness, the anger against his family, the futility of life. But none of that would bother him. Not now. For these few moments, the drugs would help. They would give him relief as they sucked away his dignity and buried him deeper in the hole that had already become impossible to climb out of.

Where mob justice left off, legal justice took over. Police arrested Daniel on more than five occasions, sending him to juvenile detention. Juvenile was a slum within a slum. Gang members. Drug dealers. Thieves. People like Daniel. The trouble was, Daniel did not have his gang for protection on the inside. He was alone. He was more at risk in Juvenile than on the street.

Evenings in Juvenile were the worst. During the day he could keep a constant watch for trouble. But at night things got serious. The setting sun brought with it a tide of evil. The shadows had faces. If he could have grown eyes in the back of his head it would have been useful.

There was no place to hide. His bed was no source of refuge. They could grab him out of bed if they wanted to. Or wait for him after, or during, his shower. The older prisoners. The men who ran the joint. The men who did what they wanted, when they wanted, and with whom they wanted. And some nights it was sex. And some nights it was with Daniel.

They attacked him and threatened his life if he made a sound. Not that it mattered. The guards did little to enforce the law in Juvenile, if it even existed there. The homosexuals had their way with Daniel, and when they were done they left him on the ground, naked, bloodied and shivering. Sometimes he stayed there all night, trying to recover from the ordeal and trying to remember as best he could what it once felt like to be optimistic about life.

On the outside, his gang often joined up with girls' gangs. It was an even trade. They protected the girls from other gangs, and the girls, in turn, gave the boys what they wanted. Daniel and the others, however, often got more than what they bargained for. While Daniel was fortunate in avoiding HIV/AIDS, he contracted sexually transmitted diseases on numerous occasions.

One time when Daniel discovered he had come down with an STD, he got as much heroin as he could and found an alley. He'd been victimized by a male gang only a few days earlier. He had shot up that evening to cope with the humiliation and violation. But there was a problem. The drugs weren't having the same effect they once did. He needed more drugs more often to keep the demons at bay. Whenever he came off the high, it was a desperate battle to make it through until the next hit.

He sat down with his back against a wooden fence. The glow of the full moon shone down from above. His body ached from the violence and the addiction. Memory. That crazy tool called memory. Where was that erase button that could wipe out what had happened? Where was the cancel command that would refuse those terrible events of his past from coming into the present and acting like they owned him?—which, to a degree, they did.

He didn't want the drugs. He didn't want those gorgeous, yet somewhat sick-looking, girls in the other gangs either. He didn't even want his friends, his so-called friends, from his own gang. He had had enough. A young man can only take so much, especially when the future looks identical to the past.

Daniel didn't want any more.

He just wanted a gun.

It didn't matter who would pull the trigger. It could be anyone. He could even do it himself. Either way, it would be done. The sickness. The drugs. The gang-raping. Everything. It could be over. It could finally be over. A gun. That's it. That's all it would take. He could get one. He could get one tonight. He knew people. He knew where to find one. One gun. One bullet. Tonight.

"Hello," a voice from the street said.

Daniel's body twitched in a nervous response. He was by himself. That was bad news. It was evening. That was worse. His body had been through enough. Not tonight. Not again.

"Are you all right?"

That was different. That was a whole lot different than what the mob said after they beat him. It was different from what the gangs said after they were through with him.

"I am here to help you. Can I help you?"

Daniel turned to see who it was. He'd never seen him before. If he was a policeman, he wasn't wearing a uniform. Just a medium-sized, medium-build, average-looking man walking into a dark alley alone at night.

"I saw you here, and you are all by yourself. Is everything all right?"

As a matter of fact, no, everything was not all right with Daniel. At the moment, *nothing* was right with Daniel.

"Who are you?" Daniel asked, still wondering if perhaps there was a group behind him ready to attack.

The man came closer. Daniel could see his face. He wasn't from the street. Couldn't be. His eyes had something in them that told Daniel he was from a place far, far from the street life. Best of all, the man was alone.

"My name is Charles Mulli."

Daniel had never heard the name before. "Mulli?"

"Yes. I would like to help you. What can I do for you?"

Do you have a gun? I could really use a gun.

"Do you live on the street?"

Daniel nodded.

"You are an orphan then."

Daniel made no reply. He didn't need to.

"I was abandoned when I was a child. My parents left me when I was six years old."

Six years old and without parents. Daniel had heard this story before.

"I had to beg for food," Charles continued. "I hated my parents for leaving me. I felt so embarrassed. I had no money. I had no food. I couldn't even go to school. But one day I heard about Jesus. When I went to a church, I heard that Jesus loves me."

Christians. Daniel had heard of them. They were the people who cursed at kids like him from their shiny cars on the way home from church.

"Jesus changed my life. I know that you are desperate, and I know that Jesus loves you and wants to change your life, too."

"My life? Change my life?" Change didn't exist for Daniel. He'd never known it.

"Yes. And I want to be your father. I want to take you to a new home where you will have food and clothing and a warm place to sleep. I want to do that for you."

It took weeks for Charles to build a trust with Daniel. They met on the streets and often talked until late in the evening, sometimes until three o'clock in the morning. Charles brought food for the gang members and told them stories about Jesus. Daniel and the fourteen other gang members accepted Charles' invitation to come to the church property in Eldoret. There they met other street kids and played games, sang songs, listened to stories about Jesus and learned to plant vegetables. Best of all, they were given a warm and safe place to sleep in a small house on the church property. Some nights Daniel snuck away to get drugs from the streets. But the longer he listened to the stories about Jesus, the less he needed to answer to those desires.

He met Esther and felt her compassion with every meal she cooked for him and his gang. She had such a welcoming attitude. The guards in Juvenile had thrown bowls of food at them. It was their job. It was their duty, and their expressions proved it. But Esther glowed. She loved this.

Somehow she loved cooking for children who could never repay her for what she was doing.

During the ensuing weeks and months, Daniel felt what it was like to be in a house jammed full of children and to be loved from wall to wall in spite of everything that he had been through.

Daniel did well in school. He completed secondary school and then went on to study sociology, where he had plans to do a master's. He gave his life to Christ and soon after felt a desire to make things right with his mother. He made the twelve-hour journey from Ndalani to his mother's home. She had moved several times, but MCF had managed to trace where she was now living to make it possible for Daniel to see her. He found the small mud house. He knocked on the door. He put his hand on the handle. Even after all these years, after all he had been through, he still had that nervous apprehension of entering his mother's house.

"Hello?"

A woman looked up at him. It had been ten years. He recognized her. But from his early teens to early twenties Daniel had changed too much, and his mother had a difficult time placing him.

"Mother?"

She looked closer at him. His voice. She recognized his voice.

"Mother, it's me. Daniel."

She got up and cried. Instead of hitting him, she gave him a hug. Instead of shouting an angry slur at him, she called out his name. They embraced for a while, not saying anything. Not needing to. His stepfather came later and hugged him as well.

Daniel stayed with them for a week. They apologized the entire time for how poorly they had treated him and for all the harm they had caused in his life.

"Mr. and Mrs. Mulli truly are your family," they told him. "They deserve to be your true parents."

As he left his biological parents, he remembered the day he had run away from home to the streets, with those crazy ideas that street life would be a dream come true. He remembered the time he met Charles while sitting in that back alley where he wanted to end it all. He remembered the day he gave his life to Christ, making it possible to forgive his parents for what had happened. And as he got onto the crowded bus to go home to Ndalani, he wondered where his life would take him and how he might be able to help people just like himself.

CHAPTER 34

Charles saw a great need for rehabilitating street girls. Many of them had been sexually abused or involved in prostitution. The problem was rampant throughout Kenya and, like the street children problem, Charles would only be able to help a few at a time. But rescuing these girls would require a new property. The girls most at risk were between sixteen and seventeen, and if taken to the Ndalani site would pose a significant temptation for the boys, not to mention the problems associated with sharing their stories with the younger girls. So Charles decided to pray for a way to help these girls.

All he needed was money, people and a location.

In 2001, Charles walked in the Ya-Ya Centre mall in Nairobi to do some shopping. As he walked out of a store, a man came up to him with a quizzical expression on his face.

"Mr. Mulli? Are you Charles Mulli?"

Charles stopped. He'd never met the man before.

"Yes, I am."

The man introduced himself. "I've heard of you. I have a plot of land in Ndalani. I would like to sell it to you very cheaply."

Charles thanked the man, and as they parted he thought about whether that particular property would suit them.

Then he got a phone call from a former government employee who worked as an assistant to a minister. Charles remembered that he had come to MCF Ndalani earlier and had been thoroughly impressed.

"I have a 200-acre property in the Yatta division. Not far from you.

Maybe twenty kilometres. I want to sell you 100 acres of that property. Could you use it?"

Charles knew the property, and yes, he could use it. It was ideal in that it was far from any major settlement, which was good for the girls. Besides, it had beautiful rolling hills that stretched out for miles.

"We are interested in the property," Charles said, "but we do not have the money at this time. Please call again in two weeks."

Two weeks later the former government employee called back. Charles told him they still didn't have the money but asked him to be patient. Everything about the property felt right. It would be perfect for the girls. It would be an incredible opportunity to get some of them off the streets and teach them skills and the word of God to change their lives in every aspect.

Charles had already laid out an idea for a program, and teachers had already expressed interest in taking part. All that was left was the money.

A few days later Charles got an email from a man overseas who wanted to donate some money to MCF. The amount was 40 percent of what was required for the property. The gift carried with it no designation, so Charles wrote back and inquired if he could use it for the Yatta project. "Use it however you want!" he wrote back. And with that, Charles phoned the former minister, telling him he had a down payment and would pay out the balance over the course of one year. Charles had no repayment plan in place. MCF was, as always, strapped for financial resources. But Charles had confidence that God was going to provide and went ahead to have the lawyers draft up the sale.

As soon as the deposit was accepted, they began the development on the property. By the end of the year God had brought in enough money each month to make all the required payments. By 2003, the former minister saw what Charles was doing and gave him the remaining 100 acres of the property.

MCF started by constructing metal-siding classrooms, dormitories and a dining area, with plans to replace them in the future with stone buildings. Teams of people from around the world, including Holland, Germany, the United States, Australia and Canada, saw the need in Yatta and raised money to help their efforts.

Charles could now spend time in the slums looking for girls who were victims of prostitution. He had a reputation for helping the street boys, and this convinced twelve girls, aged fifteen to twenty-one, to trust him and leave their dangerous occupations for a chance to learn new skills at MCF Yatta.

Charles drove them from the slum to the site and turned down the winding road. When they reached the site, Charles stopped the van and showed the girls their new home. A place without danger. A place without fear. A place where they could receive without having to put themselves at risk.

He took them on a tour, showing them their new sleeping accommodations and the classrooms.

"We have special programs for you to choose from. We can offer you training in dressmaking, hairdressing, carpentry, microfinance to start your own business, home economics including cooking, baking and childcare, and we also offer a course in missions in the event you decide after your three-year stay here that you want to reach other people with the love of Christ, even as you have been reached with it."

The girls couldn't believe it. They had nothing. No skills. No money. No means with which to pay him back. Yet somehow this man had decided to give them every opportunity to change their lives from a wretched nightmare to a bright hope.

Their daily program in the all-women's school consisted of Bible studies and learning their specific trade. They had extra activities, like choir, drama, dancing and sports. With each week they developed increasing confidence in their relationship with Christ, enabling them to see the difference between who they had been and who they were now. They all excelled at what they had chosen. When visitors came, they were eager to show off samples of their dressmaking achievements. The choirs sang for them, conveying their deep-seated joy that they were once lost but had been found.

Charles drove home from the Yatta site, having preached to women about God's unconditional forgiveness. "No matter where you've been," he told them, "you have never gone too far for God."

He got back to the Ndalani site in time to hear the end of their daily evening program. When he came to the front, he greeted them with his classic *Ooo-aye*. The children clapped and cheered for him. He brought greetings from their brothers and sisters in Eldoret and their new family members in Yatta.

"Our family is growing," Charles said. "We are now more than seven hundred."

That brought more clapping and cheers.

"Some of you came from the streets where you had no one. Now you have me as your father and," he pointed to Esther, "you have a mother. And you have so many brothers and sisters. Do you see how much God loves you?"

He prayed for them and then dismissed them.

When the crowd dispersed, Charles found one of those rare times in his life when he could stop and enjoy the quiet night air. He stood under the metal roof that was supported by wood posts. There were no walls, which allowed every bug imaginable to come inside. At the other end of the assembly area, a young man who had come to MCF to volunteer for a few months finished talking with some of his students. Over the years, MCF was blessed to have hundreds of volunteers from all around the world for various lengths of stay to help in whatever way was needed. As the students hurried off to their evening study time, he approached Mr. Mulli.

"Mr. Mulli?"

Charles turned to face him. With his soft voice and genuine smile he reached out his hand to shake the young man's hand. He called him by name and asked him how he was.

"I'm fine," he said. "And you?"

"It has been a great day. I was in Yatta, today."

"How are things going there?"

"They are going well. God has been so good to us. So good to us."

"I heard the story of how all the money came together for Yatta. It's amazing."

"Yes, it is."

"Mr. Mulli, do you ever worry the finances aren't going to come through? That's a lot to ask of God—all that money, the property, the volunteers. How did you know it was going to work out?"

Charles smiled. "That is a good question. You know, the hardest thing to do is to ask people for money. It's strange, but the success has come not through pleading with people for money but by God working in people to give to the ministry. People whose hearts are changed give freely. And when they give, they are happy about it."

"It seems like it works out for you every time," the young man replied. "For others of us, trusting God for big things is a scary prospect. At least it is for me. I just don't always think God is going to come through for me."

"The critical thing is faith. The belief that God will provide. I ask myself the question—why am I doing what I'm doing? Is it for me, or is it for God? And whether you are in ministry or in business or whatever you are doing, that's the same question for all of us."

A fat bug landed in the young man's ear. He swatted at it, showing obvious frustration. Charles laughed.

"I see you haven't gotten used to the bugs yet," he said.

The young man swatted again to make sure the bug was gone.

"Can I ask you another question?" he asked.

"Of course," Charles replied.

"I'm curious about what you think of prosperity. I've heard people define that word different ways. And I always wondered why there is such an emphasis on it. Since I've come here, I've met kids who have nothing. All of their possessions fit in a little box. Most of them have one or two sets of clothes. They have old shoes and practically no possessions. Yet they are far happier than we are. Just the other evening when the rain was pouring down, I was lying down in my bunk bed with the mosquito netting all around me. I looked over and saw my little bag that contained all my travelling possessions. I had to take it off the ground and put it on the table so the rainwater that was seeping in wouldn't soak it."

Charles laughed again. "The rain does come in sometimes."

"As I lay there in my bed it occurred to me that I have never been happier in all my life."

"That's great."

"It made me wonder about the concept of prosperity and what the purpose of it is. You've seen it all. The poverty, the wealth, the poor, the rich, the sick, the healthy, the orphans, the rescued children. Everything. I'm curious. How do you define prosperity?"

"That is a good question." Charles leaned up against one of the unstable posts and swatted a bug away. "What is prosperity?" He became quiet and it seemed as though he was thinking through everything he had lived through before he came up with a response. "Most people will disagree with me on this. But for me, prosperity is a changed life."

The young man had never heard of that before. Here was Charles Mulli, an abandoned child who became extremely successful only to give it all away to help those who were just like he had been. He had experienced what it meant to have no prosperity, what it meant to have prosperity in abundance and what it meant to share every last bit of his prosperity with others. And yet, his definition of prosperity had nothing to do with money or possessions.

"A changed life?"

"If a person from the street gives their life to Christ and then decides to help other people, that is prosperity. They've gone from the street to a place where God can use them. But if somebody who already has money gets more of it, how is that prosperity? If someone who has enough to eat, who has enough clothing, if all they do is get more of it, how is that prosperity? I see it differently. If someone is demon possessed and gets freed so they can study and live the way God wants them to, that is prosperity. If someone is a prostitute who is being taken advantage of, sometimes even by their own family, and they are freed from that to live for Christ, this, too, is prosperity. Their life is changed. This is prosperity."

The young man said nothing. He felt the way people do when they've been given an answer that is both too deep and too simple to comprehend at one time. He nodded his head. Charles smiled and said goodbye as he left to catch up on some of his remaining work.

Prosperity is a changed life.

For years to come that line never left the young man.

CHAPTER 35

Charles got up early in the morning. It was still dark. Only the cooks were up. It was cool outside—but the sun would soon change that. He walked past the dormitories, thinking of the hundreds of children sleeping inside. How do fifteen years go by so fast? He passed by Jacob's Well, God's providential supply of water. The well outlived its usefulness and had been replaced with an eighty-metre borehole on the other side of the site. But the truth that God performs miracles still lived on in the children who were there the day the workers got ready to dig in a place where there wasn't supposed to be any water.

We've come a long way, You and I, Charles prayed. *You have delivered over 700 children out of poverty, out of the streets, out of danger. You have done mighty miracles, God. You have healed the sick. You have destroyed the power of Satan in these children's lives. You have provided food. You have blessed our farms such that we are able to export half of our produce to earn money for MCF. And LORD, You have given the vision for this mission to people around the world. Thank You for our friends. Thank You for their passion in reaching the orphans. Without them this would not be possible. Bless them in their lives.*

This week, we are celebrating the fifteen-year anniversary of Mully Children's Family. I still recall that moment on the highway when You called me. And look where we are now. We have done quite a lot. Thank You for using me in this way. It is a privilege to be used of You to do this. I pray that the celebrations today will bring honour to You. For You are the reason we are here.

Charles received letters from his supporters all over Europe, Australia and North America. Some had been with him for years. Others had joined more recently. Yet they all had the same desire to reach out to a hurting world through Mully Children's Family.

Together with volunteers, teachers and students from MCF, Charles went into the Kipsongu slum to minister to children. Charles had been here numerous times before and had rescued children, some of whose parents still lived in the same huts. They got out of the van and walked to a collection of huts. Those who were new to the slums felt the insecurity that comes with being around poverty and crime. Everything looked grey. Huts made of used garbage bags dotted the pathetic landscape. Shaky dwelling units made of sheet metal, plywood or cardboard lined the streets. The ground acted both as a road and a sewer. There were no latrines. The smell forced some of the newcomers to breathe through their mouths. Charles had long since gotten used to it. He shook hands with people, scanning the crowd and the area behind them for children who were at death's door. Two boys sat on the side of the road. They wore torn and oily T-shirts. Their faces were dirty. They had no shoes. Charles greeted those whom he knew. He'd been here many times before, which was good, because the relationships he had built gave him credibility and security in the normally dangerous slum environment.

People gathered around them as they began to hand out food. The MCF team handed out vegetables and fruits. After they ate, Charles gave a message—never an easy thing to do with people who are on the verge of starvation.

As the team talked with some of the people afterwards, Charles' attention was diverted to a young boy standing off by himself in the distance. The longer he looked at him, the more familiar he became. He'd seen him before. One of Charles' friends on the team recognized the boy, too. The boy looked up. He remembered them.

His name was Michael, and he was one who straddled that unpredictable line between life and death.

Charles walked towards him. They had been looking for him for quite some time. Michael hadn't changed. Same ripped shirt. Same ragged pants. Same worried look on his face that improved somewhat when he saw Charles and his friends coming towards him. They knelt down and gave Michael a big hug. The boy's rancid odour seeped through onto Charles' shirt. His face was a mess from snot running out of his nose. His eyes were puffy, a sign of his five-year-old body's inability to keep up with the attack of diseases.

"Hello, Michael," Charles said.

Those words felt so good to Michael. He felt the passion in Charles' eyes. He'd heard the rumours about Charles Mulli. He'd heard about that place where kids went when this very man came to give them a future. A place with beds. A place with a school. A place with food. With friends. With safety. With love. With Christ.

Charles' friends volunteered to sponsor Michael to go to MCF. One of them had seen him before on her previous visit to MCF. When she had returned home, Michael's presence remained as near as if she had never left Kipsongu slum.

And in a way, she hadn't.

Like the hundreds of volunteers from around the world who had come to MCF, she took the compassion of caring for the children back home, resulting in a renewed interest to continue supporting MCF and help impoverished people around the world.

They left Kipsongu slum, bringing Michael, as well as two others, with them. He looked out of the van window, feeling the anticipation of a new life. As they took the turn off the main road onto the MCF Ndalani property, he saw the children, his new brothers and sisters, playing football on the field. They drove down to the school site and showed him his dormitory. Thanks to countless fundraising efforts of MCF supporters, Charles presented Michael with a new bunk bed, complete with a mattress and a blanket.

"This is my new home?" Michael asked.

"This is it. What do you think?" Charles sat down next to him on his bed, feeling relieved Michael was still alive and being thankful that he was now in a safe place.

Michael smiled. "I like it here. I like it here a lot."

Another MCF child came in and introduced himself to Michael. Together they hurried off to explore the property.

Michael woke up that morning an orphan. But he went to bed as a member of a family.

The next day Charles and an MCF team visited a juvenile remand home, a state-sponsored facility for homeless children. In an effort to keep these children off the street, the Kenyan government sent them to one of hundreds of underfinanced places like this one in an effort to contain them. The demand on the Kenyan government was too great, making it impossible for them to provide the care these children required. In this particular home, eighty-five children shared small quarters with no blankets or mattresses.

Under instructions not to touch them or make contact with them, the team handed out warm stew and chapatti bread to the children, who had that curious appearance of being both beautiful and desperate. As Charles and the team got back into the van, they looked back at the children being taken back into their accommodations. It was better than living on the street. Still, it did nothing to shake the feeling of hurt Charles felt, knowing that in spite of having given his life to help this problem, there was far, far more to do than what had already been done.

At MCF Ndalani, the team faced the challenge of using donated medical kits to test the children for HIV/AIDS. The team drew blood from each child and mixed it with a solution to determine which children had contracted the virus. They waited those eternal three minutes for each test to indicate which children were healthy and which were not. Of the 713 children tested, 79 had HIV/AIDS.

Thousands of people came to MCF Ndalani in 2004 to join in *Celebrating Fifteen Years of God's Wondrous Grace and Miracles*. It was the end of a week-long celebration that included work in the slums, open-air meetings in Eldoret, handing out food and supplies to the community and giving testimonies. As one of the MCF children's choirs sang for the massive crowd, Charles walked to the back of the audience to be with his parents, Daudi and Rhoda. They had since become active participants in the ministry, working alongside their son in rescuing the children of the streets.

"You have done well, Charles," Daudi said. "This is incredible. Absolutely incredible."

"God continues to do a mighty work here, doesn't He?"

Daudi nodded his head. He turned to look at Charles. They made eye contact.

"Thank you Charles," Daudi said. "Thank you for everything."

Charles put his arm around his father and listened as the children began their next song.

Later that evening, after all the cleanup was finished, Charles stood with Esther, looking out on the property. The stars flooded the night sky. Some of the younger children were already in bed. Some of the older ones talked with each other as they made their way to the dormitories.

Charles and Esther didn't say anything. They didn't have to. It was all right in front of them. They stood together in silence, feeling the reward that comes to people who stick together through good, difficult and unexpected circumstances.

Esther went in for the night. Charles watched as she unlocked the door to their small metal-siding dwelling. He could just as soon have been watching her enter some brand new home of theirs. Had he hung on to those businesses, he could have afforded a gorgeous mansion for her. Cars. Clothes. Vacations. Everything. But those thoughts did not enter his mind. Not any more. He had long since crossed over that bridge. Instead, he took in a deep breath and felt the sense of purpose that resulted from risking everything for God.

He got into bed. Esther was already asleep. What a day.

What a life.

In those quiet moments before he drifted off, he thought about the adventures he had shared with God, about the children that now had a future and about the hundreds of people who had given their lives to Christ. As he lay there in the still of the evening, he remembered many of the good things that had happened in these fifteen years and wondered about the good things yet to come.

It was the best time of day.

CASTLE QUAY BOOKS

For more information and to explore the rest of our titles visit

www.castlequaybooks.com